Bhajan Supplement 2020

Volume 2

Mata Amritanandamayi Center
San Ramon, California, USA

Bhajan Supplement 2020 – Volume 2

Published By:
Mata Amritanandamayi Center
P.O. Box 613
San Ramon, CA 94583-0613, USA

In India:
www.amritapuri.org
inform@amritapuri.org

In Europe:
www.amma-europe.org

In US:
www.amma.org

About Pronunciation

The following key is for the guidance of those who are unfamiliar with the transliteration codes used in this book:

A	-as	a	in America
AI	-as	ai	in aisle
AU	-as	ow	in how
E	-as	e	in they
I	-as	ea	in heat
O	-as	o	in or
U	-as	u	in suit
KH	-as	kh	in Eckhart
G	-as	g	in give
GH	-as	gh	in loghouse
PH	-as	ph	in shepherd
BH	-as	bh	in clubhouse
TH	-as	th	in lighthouse
DH	-as	dh	in redhead
CH	-as	ch-h	in staunch-heart
JH	-as	dge	in hedgehog
Ñ	-as	ny	in canyon
Ṣ	-as	sh	in shine
Ś	-as	c	in efficient
Ṅ	-as	ng	in sing (nasal sound)
V	-as	v	in valley
ZH	-as	rh	in rhythm
R	-as	r	in ride

Vowels with a line on top are pronounced like the vowels listed above but held twice as long.
The letters with dots under them (ṭ, ṭh, ḍ, ḍh, ṇ) are palatal sounds. They are pronounced with the tip of the tongue against the hard palate.

Table of Contents of 3 the Volumes

abhayaṅkarī ammē (Malayalam)

abhayaṅkarī ammē suravanditē
hṛdayēśvari ammē vidhipūjitē

O Mother, giver of fearlessness, you are worshipped by the gods. O Mother, Goddess of our heart, worshipped by Lord Brahma!

makkaḷām ñaṅgaḷil kṛpa-tūkaṇē
māyatan valayil akapeṭṭu pōyi
akṣīṇam ñaṅgaḷ śramikkunnu ammē
vāsanakaḷ tīrttu rakṣikkaṇē

Please shower your grace upon us, Your children. Caught in the net of illusion, we are working tirelessly to escape. O Mother, please put an end to our vasanas (tendencies of our mind) and save us!

aham-enna bōdhattil āzhnniṭum enne
kṛpatūki ninnil cērttīṭaṇē
ōmkārattin poruḷē ammē
ōmkāra nādamāyi māṭṭukenne

I drown in the identification to 'I' and 'mine'. Please shower Your grace upon me, draw me close to you. O Mother, who are the very essence of the syllable Om, please make me one with the sound Om!

śraddhayum bhaktiyum ennil uṇarnniṭān
nityam namikkunnu nin padam ñān
ammē nin ānanda sāgaram pūkiṭān
ēzhayām enne anugrahikkū

For faith and devotion to awaken within me, I ever bow at your feet. O Mother, please bless this helpless one, that I may reach your ocean of bliss!

akataḷiril aṭimalar (Malayalam)

akataliril aṭimalar teḷiññu kaṇḍīṭuvān
anavaratam akhilēśī aṭiyan uzhalunnu
atinoriṭa taruvatinu maṙayāy varunnat-en
aṙivētumiyalāymayāluḷḷa karmamō?

O Goddess of the universe, I constantly yearn to see your lotus feet clearly in my heart. Are my unwise actions veiling my vision?

amaratva-bōdhattil uṇaruvatināy en
akhila-karmaṅgaḷum aviṭuttatāy ñān
aniśam arppiccaṭi paṇitu nilkkumbōḷ
akatārin teḷinīril aviṭunnu teḷiyum

I offer all my actions at your feet, that I may awaken to the knowledge of immortality. As I totally surrender to You, please appear clearly within the pure waters of my heart.

apatha-sañcārattāl aṭipataṙiṭāte
akamanam akamukhamāy mātram carikkān
atisaraḷam-anunimiṣam-agrē gamikkān
ahaituka-kṛpāsindhō! kūppunnu nityam

Let my feet not stray to the wrong path. Let my mind be introverted and only move inward. Let me easily move forward continually. For this, I pray to You, O ocean of inexplicable grace!

aruḷ-mozhikaḷ koṇḍ-aṭiyan arutāymayokkevē
atijīvanam ceytu aṙiyumā satyam
aṙivutān ñān enna bōdham uṇarumbōḷ
aṙiyuvān illonnum aṙivu tān eṅgum

Your loving words will guide me to transcend all wrongs and reach the Truth. When I realize that I am transcendental awareness, then nothing will remain to be known. There is only pure awareness everywhere.

āli paṭarum (Malayalam)

āli paṭarum apāra-śōkāgniyil
āzhnnu pōkunnu ñān ammē
āzhnnu pōkunnu ñān

Oh Mother, the raging fires of unending grief engulf me.

tāpāgni jvālakaḷ tāzhān
nin snēhattin tūmazha tūkāttat-entē

Won't you extinguish these roaring flames with a shower of Your Love?

āzham-ērum bhava-śōkārṇṇavattinde
nīrāvi nīḷe-paṭarnnū

Sorrow rises up like water vapor from this bottomless ocean of samsara and spreads everywhere.

vyōma-dēśaṅgaḷum bhūmiyum māññu pōy
tīram innētum tiriyā ammē
tīram innētum tiriyā

Earth and sky have disappeared and still I have not reached the shore, O Mother.

yāciccituṇnu ñān snēhārdra-mānasē
tāvaka-anugrahāśissu nēṭān

O Mother, your soft heart is ever intent on showering love. I am begging for your blessing.

āvirānanda prakāśam
parattu nin cēvaḍittāratil ñān aliyān ammē
cēvaḍittāratil ñān aliyān

Shed your infinite light, let me merge in your lotus feet!

aisā dil (Hindi)

aisā dil dēnā dēvī
jan sēvā kar sakē
mōh andhēr kō taj kē
śraddhā jōt jalā sakē

O Devi, give me a heart that wants to serve all. May I renounce the darkness of attachments. Please light the flame of faith and awareness.

aisā prēm bahānā dēvī
sab kō apnā sakē
bhēd-bhāv kō chōḍ kē
har dil se juḍ sakē

Let such a love flow, O Devi, that I may be able to enfold all in it, and give up all differences. May my heart be one with every other.

sarvēṣām svastir bhavatu, sarvēṣām śāntir bhavatu

May all be healthy, may all be peaceful.

aisā bal dēnā dēvī
aham bhāv kō tyāg sakē
piñjrā svārtth kā chōḍ kē
cidākāś mēṅ uḍ sakē

Give me strength, O Devi, to renounce all sense of ego. Help me break away from the cage of selfishness, and fly free in the vast pure consciousness.

akumu no youna (Japanese)

akumu no youna genjitsuk ni
zetsubou shite ilu hitobito
kasaneta tsumi o yulushite
shukufuku shite kudasalu okata

This world seems like a bad dream, and people are driven to despair. O bestower of grace, I beg Your forgiveness for all my transgressions.

sotto hitomi o tojileba
amma no okao ga ukabu
amma amma amma amma
amma amma amma amma

I close my eyes gently, and Amma's divine countenance appears.

ikari to kanashimi o tolisali
kurushimi o sukutte kudasalu
ataelalelu shifuku
subete no souzou sri shitti

It is you who remove my anger and sorrow, and rescue me from suffering. O bestower of bliss, Sri Siddhi, goddess of all creation!

watashi wa kokoro dewa nai
watashi wa karada dewa nai
watashi wa junsui ishiki kagayaku

I am neither the body, nor the mind. I am pure awareness.

ambā gauri (Hindi)

ambā gauri jagajanani kis pal tūhe sōtī
āṅsū hamārē tērē liyē kabhi phūl kabhi mōti

O Mother of the world, when do You sleep? We offer you our tears as flowers and pearls.

ham hai phūl tēri bagiyā kē
sīñc rahi tu dhīraj sē
prēmamayi hamē khud sā banādē
bhar dē hamē karuṇā sē

We are flowers in Mother's garden. Mother watches over us with patience as we grow. Embodiment of love, Mother, please make us like You, and fill us with compassion.

mā ambē gauri janani
naman tērē caraṇōṅ mēṅ

O Mother, we offer our salutations at Your feet.

ham nē śitaltā hai pāyi
tēri gōd mēṅ jananī
ō ammā tu prēm ki gaṅgā
tū nit sahaj hi bahati

In Your lap, we experience the coolness of Your divine love. Mother is the Ganga of divine love that flows spontaneously.

dē hamkō bhī aisi matī mā
prēm sandēś phailāyē
mīṭhā bōlē ik muskān sē
sab kō sukh pahuṅcāyē

Please grant us a mind that spreads the message of love. May we spread joy through sweet words and loving smiles.

ambā jananī (Sanskrit)

ambā jananī abhirāmī
abhayapradāyini śivakāmini
ambā jananī sarveśvarī
śāntasvarūpiṇi śivaśaṅkari

satyasvarūpiṇi śrīmātā
śāśvatānanda dāyini mā
jagadīśvari śaśiśēkharē
nirvāṇadāyini dēvī mā

ambā jay jay mā
jagadambā jay jay mā
mā jay mā jay mā jay mā

ambā kāḷī (Sanskrit)

ambā kāḷī jagadamba kāḷī
ammā kāḷī bhadra kāḷī
ammē kāḷī bhavāni kāḷī
ammē kāḷī durgā kāḷī

mahiṣāsura marddini ammā kāḷī
bhakta-rakṣaki devī amme kāḷī
nāsābharaṇa bhāsurā dēvī kāḷī
hṛdayanivāsini ammē kāḷī

puṣpavarṣiṇi dēvi ammē kāḷī
sarva-maṅgaḷa-kāriṇi ammā kāḷī
kārunyāmṛta-varṣiṇi dēvi kāḷī
amṛtānandamayi dēvi kāḷī

ambā kṛpā varṣām (Sanskrit)

ambā kṛpā varṣām karōtu
jagadamba kṛpā varṣām karōtu
sarvāṇi karmāṇi samyak kartum
guru sēvā bhāvam dadātu mē

Mother, please shower your grace. Mother of the world, please shower your grace. Please bless me with the attitude of guru seva so that I may do all actions properly.

tava nētrē snēham snigdhāpāṅgam
madhura vacanam śrutvā manasi śāntir bhavati
sarvāḥ duḥkhāḥ manasaḥ gachanti
ō mātā gurumātā sṛṣṭē hē mūlam

Your eyes are full of binding love. Hearing your sweet voice fills my mind with peace. All sorrows disappear from my mind, O mother, mother Guru, root of creation.

lōkāḥ samastāḥ sukhinō bhavantu
idam varam dadātu mē ō mātā jagadambā
śānti puṣpāṇām vṛṣṭim ca snēham ca
bhavitum kṛpa varṣām karōtu idam

"May all beings in the world be happy." Please grant me this boon, O mother of the world. For a shower of flowers of love and peace, please shower your grace.

ammā ammā ammā (Tamil)

ammā ammā ammā ammā enakku piḍitta ammā
ammā ammā ammā ammā entan cella ammā
ammā ammā ammā ammā piriyā varam vēṇḍum
ammā ammā ammā ammā anpu muttam ammā

Amma, my loving Amma! Amma, my darling Amma! Amma, grant me the boon of never leaving you! Amma, loving kisses to You!

enakku piḍitta narumaṇam ammā untan narumaṇam
enakku piḍitta nimiḍam ammā untan darisanam
enakku piḍitta kāṭccī ammā untan tiruvuruvam

Amma, Your fragrance is my favorite fragrance. Your darshan is my favorite moment. Your divine form is my favorite sight.

enakku piḍitta uṇavu ammā untan prasādam
enakku piḍitta ōsai ammā untan tēnmōzhi
enakku piḍitta sēyal atu ammā untan tiruppaṇi

Your prasad is my favorite food. Your sweet words are my favorite sounds. Doing seva for You is my favorite activity

ammā ammā ammā ammā, ammā dēvi ammā
ammā ammā ammā ammā, ammā kāḷi ammā

ammā dēvi jagadīśvari (Sanskrit)

ammā dēvi jagadīśvari
karuṇāmayi dēvi hṛdayēśvarī

sarvēśvari māhēśvari
paramēśvari bhuvanēśvari

śāntipradāyini puṣpavarṣiṇi
śōkavināśini abhayaṅkari
ānandadāyini bhairavi mā
bhavabhaya bhañjini bhārgavi mā

prēmasvarūpiṇi jagajjanani
ātmaprakāśini ādiśakti
mākāra-rūpiṇi pārvati mā
ōmkāra-rūpini sarasvati mā

tripurasundari śvētāmbari
hṛdayavāsini sanātani
sumandahāsini kāḷī mā
pādāmbujam namaḥ sadguru mā

Amma devi ma (French)

amma devi ma
tu es celle qui sait
amma devi ma
tu es celle qui connait

O Mother Devi, You are the one who is aware. You are the one who knows everything.

devi ma devi ma
devi ma devi ma

amma devi ma
tu es en chacun
amma devi ma
tu es le trésor

O Mother Devi, You are in all. Mother Devi, you are the treasure.

amma devi ma
reine de l'univers
amma devi ma
montre la lumière

Mother Devi, queen of the Universe! Mother Devi, show me light.

Amma Du bist mein (German)

Amma Du bist mein
zeig mir wie werd ich Dein
Amma, Du bist mein
und ich bin Dein

Amma you are mine. Show me how to become Yours. Amma, You are mine and I am Yours.

Ganz Dein Eigen will ich sein
komm zeig mir wie werd ich Dein

I want to be Yours entirely. Please show me how to become Yours.

Alle Gedanken, Worte und Taten
weih ich Dir, gehör nur Dir
Ein frohes Reigen ist's mit uns beiden!
Komm halte mich, bleibe immer bei mir!

I offer to You all my thoughts, words and deeds. I belong only to You. Happily we dance a circle dance. Please hold me. Stay with me always.

Ohne Dich finde ich gar keinen Sinn
Du weist mir den Weg ins Licht
Im Tanz des Lebens schenkst Du mir Liebe
Bringst mich ans Ziel, ja das weiss ich gewiss

Without you, there is no meaning. Show me the path to light. In the dance of life, You shower love on me and bring me to the goal. Yes I know this clearly.

jai ma jai ma jai jai ma
jai ma jai ma jai jai ma

Amma, hoy me siento lejos (Spanish)

Amma, hoy me siento lejos,
Lejos, tan lejos de tí
dolor me abruma, Me quema y me esfuma

Amma, today I feel so far from You. That pain overwhelms me, burns me, consumes me.

O madre de amor o madre de mi corazón

O mother of love, O mother of my heart!

Escucho tu voz en el silencio
de mi corazón Yo nunca te olvido
Mi niña, mi niño querida querido
Yo siempre estoy contigo

In the silence of my heart, I hear Your voice: “My darling I never forget you. My darling child, my darling child, I’m always with you.”

Eres mi consuelo, mi compañía
mi aliento, mi pensamiento
Eres lo lleno, lo vacío
el silencio de mi corazon

Amma You are my comfort, my company, my breath, my thought. Amma You are the full and the empty. Amma You are the silence of my heart.

Amma mother of my heart (English)

Amma... Mother of my heart and soul,
Amma... my very life, my path and goal.
Amma... You have showered us with grace.
Amma... Please don't take your love away.

Amme devi bhagavati, Amme devi,
Amme devi bhagavati, mother of my heart and soul.

The universe with all it's stars, is just a bubble that we see.
Your divine and smiling face that lasts through all eternity--
how can I worship Amma completely?
With your grace, then surely you will teach me.

Like a million milky ways that pour their heaven down to earth,

your supreme reality [that] transcends even death and birth.
Let me always bow down before you.
With a wish, we always will adore you.

Amma my heart (English)

Amma my heart is not filled
with love and compassion.
With your grace, may it happen.

Remove our selfish thoughts
and the darkness from our mind.
With your darshan, give us devotion.

Show us the true path.
Come into our hearts
and light the lamp of selfless service.

amma nin mugdhamām (Malayalam)

amma nin mugdhamām āliṅganattināl
nin sparśana prēma divya tīrtthattināl
ā prēmasāgara tīratt-aṇaññu ñān
ānanda bhāṣpam pozhikkum ennum – ammē

O Mother! In your loving embrace, in the love flowing from your divine touch, I have reached the shores of the ocean of your love, and I cry tears of joy.

amma nin pādattil āzhnnu kiṭakkave
enne marannu ñān rāppakalum
amma nin pādattil muruke piṭiccu ñān
aṇiyikkum innoru bhāṣpahāram

O Mother! As I lie safe at your feet, I forget myself and the days and nights. I shall cling to your feet, and adorn you with a garland of my tears.

ninnōmal kaikaḷāl enne tazhukumbōḷ
en manam ennum suśāntamākum
ellām marannorā dhanya nimiṣattil
ennum ramikkān enikku mōham

When You caress me with your gentle hands, my heart becomes bright and peaceful. I forget myself in the bliss of that blessed moment, and long to ever remain thus.

Amma okaasam (Japanese)

Amma okaasam
Amma itsumo kokoni itekudasai
Amma muneno oku ni

O my Mother, Amma, please always stay deep in my heart.

Dakishimete kono karada o koete
Sasayaite eiem no kotodama
Amma okaasam

Amma, O my Mother, embrace me beyond this body, and whisper eternal mantras to me.

Amma sono hitomino oku
Amma zutto mitsumete itaino
Amma toki o koete

Amma, I want to gaze into your eyes that are beyond time.

Michibiite yasashiku aremasu youni
Yorokobi ni michiahulete itaino
Amma okaasam

Amma, O my mother, please teach me to be compassionate! May you guide me to be blissful!

Amma arigato
Amma okaasam

Thank you, Amma, my Mother.

Amma otzmat (Hebrew)

amma otzmat haor
mitgalgelet midor le dor
ve eyna posachat aleinu kan

Amma, the power of light continues through the generations and includes everyone.

benetinat haemuna shela
mesira et kol ha pchadim
maamika shorashim refuyim
mechashelet mul hakshayim

Giving us faith, She removes all fears. She strengthens our lost roots, and empowers us in the face of challenge.

emuna ve nisim noladim yad be yad
haemuna hee ahava, ha ahava hee emuna

Faith and miracles are born hand in hand. Faith is love, love is faith.

kaasher nitatef beora
veneda et taama
nuchal lehaavir hal-a et birkata

When Her light envelopes us, we taste Her greatness. Then we can pass on Her blessings.

Amma tu danses (French)

Amma tu danses avec Krishna
Je rêve de toi en Krishna bhava
Danse avec moi, amour et joie

Amma, You dance with Krishna. I dream of You in Krishna bhava. Dance with me, O love and joy!

Amma ma ma ma amma ma ma ma
Amma ma ma ma amma ma ma

Amma, tu danses en Kali bhava
Unie à devi, Amma, tu brilles
et tes prières aident la terre

Amma, dance in Kali bhava. You shine, as one with Devi. Your prayers help the Earth.

Amma, tu danses avec le monde
Tu vois dieu partout, tu embrasses tout,
soignes et nourris les démunis

Amma, You dance with the world, seeing God everywhere. You embrace all. You heal and feed the destitute.

Amma je veux danser pour toi,
offrir la beauté et t'adorer
Enlève mes peurs, brille dans mon coeur

Amma, I want to dance for You and offer beauty. I want to adore You. Remove my fears, and shine in my heart!

amma unnai ariyāmal (Tamil)

amma unnai ariyāmal
un mahimay puriyāmal ēṅkukirēn
pala pala janmaṅgaḷ vīṇāga kazhittēn
un malaraṭi pattrikkoḷvēn

O Mother, I long for You. I have wasted many births, unable to know You or understand Your glory. Now I will hold on to Your lotus feet.

nī en vazhiyāga seyalpaṭumbōḍu
nān seydadenṭru perumai koṇḍēnē
anaittirkkum ādhāram allavō tāyē nī
en manadai tūymai seyvāyē

Though I know You alone act through me, still I take credit saying, 'I did that!' O Mother, You are the substratum of everything! Please purify my mind.

ammā... ammā... ammā... ammā...

nī kāṭṭittarum vazhi naṭappadarkku
un kaiyil pāvaiyāy ākkiṭuvāyā?

en kai piṭittu azhaittuccenṭru
ennai kaṭaittēttra vandaruḷvāyā

Please make me your instrument. Help me walk the path You show? Please hold my hand and take me to the goal?

ammā unnanbu (Tamil)

ammā unnanbu enmēl nirmmalam nittiyam
ānālum makaḷentan pāsamendrum suyanalam
unnaiviṭṭu tolaidūram nān sendrālum
unnuṭanē nānirukka uḷḷanpu vēṇḍum

O Mother! Your love for me is pure, selfless and eternal, though this daughter's love stems from her selfish ego. Even if I have to go far away from you, let my love for you be rooted deeply in my heart forever.

nī sintum punnakayin oḷiyālē
en nāḷēllām inpamāyi tīrntiṭumē
naḷḷiravil pozhiyum nilavoḷi pōl
un punnakayil en manamum oḷiperumē

The light of your smile makes my day joyful. Like a ray of moonlight on a dark night, your smile brightens my mind.

kālamellām punnagaikkāy kāttiruppēn
kāṇāmal vāṭi manam ēṅkiṭuvēn
nilaiyaṭra en anpum nilaiperavē
ammā nin tiruppādam nāṭiṭuvēn

Longing forever for your smile, my withered mind languishes, unable to behold it. Please give me steadfast love for you. O Mother, I take refuge at your holy feet.

endrendrum enakku nī uṇḍu tāyē
vazhīyamaittu vazhītuṇayāy varukirāyē
vāzhvilum tāzhvilum maravāmal – unnai
piriyāmal irukkavē aruḷvāyē

You're always here for me, guiding and protecting me in every step. Through all the highs and lows of life, bless me to remember you and stay with you.

Amma, you are everything (English)

Amma you are everything.
I can't live without you.
Shower me with grace.
Forgive me my mistakes

kali ma… kali ma… kali ma… kali ma…

Don't leave me alone.
Draw me close to you.
Grant me the boon to sleep in your arms,
and give me a place in your heart.

Let me serve the world
as an instrument in your hands.
Give me humility and devotion
and a place at your holy feet.

Amma wa itsumo (Japanese)

amma wa itsumo iru
amma ga yondeiru
hashitte amma no tokoro ni iku
utau jay jay mā, jay jay mā, jay jay mā

Amma is always everywhere. Amma is calling me. I will run to Amma. Sing victory to Amma!

moshi michini mayottara
kamisama o yonde miyo
amma ga tasukeni kitekureru
utau jay jay mā, jay jay mā, jay jay mā

When I lose my way, I call out to God. Amma will come and save me. Let us sing, "Victory to Amma"!

sekaiyo heiwani nare
subetega shiawaseni naru
amma to isshoni inorimasu
utau jay jay mā, jay jay mā, jay jay mā

I wish the whole world peace. I wish that all may be happy. I pray along with Amma. May Amma be victorious.

ammā dēvi kāḷi mā ammā dēvi kāḷi mā
ammā dēvi kāḷi mā ammā dēvi kāḷi mā

ammē abhayapradē (Malayalam)

ammē abhayapradē ātmaprakāśini nī
sarva saukhyapradē prēmasvarūpiṇi

Mother, you grant refuge and are the light of the Self. You bestow all happiness and are the embodiment of divine love.

dēhōhabōdham nī māttittarū ammē
dēvī manōharī en hṛdayēśvarī

Please remove my body identification, Mother, Devi, enchantress of all, Goddess of my heart.

janmāntaraṅgaḷāy kūḍe ñān kūṭṭiya
pāpabhāram akattū santāpanāśini

O destroyer of sorrow, please remove the burden of sin that I have gathered over lifetimes.

sadguru jagadambē vazhikāṭṭi tarēṇamē
bhaktiyum śaktiyum prēmavum ēkaṇē

O Sadguru, Mother of the world, show me the way! Please grant devotion, strength and divine love.

śuddhamākkiyen manakōvilil ennennum
jñānakkeḍāviḷakkāy jvalikkū jaganmayi

O Mother of the world! Please make the temple of my mind pure, and shine there as the lamp of knowledge, ever ablaze.

ammē ammē amṛtēśvarī (Malayalam)

ammē ammē amṛtēśvarī

O Mother, immortal goddess!

ammayenna mahāmatram uruviṭumbōḷ
niṟaññ-ozhukīṭunnu mizhikaḷ ammē

entin-ennaṙiyilla, mūkamākunnen hṛdantam
śāntamākunnen hṛdantam, tṛptamākunnen
hṛdantam

When I utter the great mantra, 'Amma,' tears flow from my eyes. I do not know why, but my heart becomes silent, calm and content.

ammē ammē hṛdayēśvarī
ammē ammē amṛtēśvarī

O Mother, goddess of my heart, O Mother, immortal goddess!

ammayenna mahāmantram smariccīṭumbōḷ
manamāke viśrānti niṙaññīṭunnu
ānanda nirvṛti nirmala vīcikaḷ
hṛdaya tantrikaḷe puṇarnnīṭunnu

As I remember the great mantra, 'Amma,' my mind attains repose and blissful purity fills my heart.

ammē ammē sarvēśvarī
ammē ammē amṛtēśvarī

O Mother, goddess of all beings; O Mother, immortal goddess!

ammayenna mahāmantram śraviccīṭumbōḷ
prēmārdram-ākunnenn-antaraṅgam
ōrō aṇuvilum ōrō kaṇattilum
tuṭiccīṭunnu nin kāruṇya spandanam

As I listen to the great mantra, 'Amma,' love fills my heart. Your compassion enlivens each atom of this universe.

ammē ammē bhuvanēśvarī
ammē ammē amṛtēśvarī

O Mother, goddess of the earth; O Mother, immortal goddess!

ammē ammē ennu (Malayalam)

ammē ammē ennu viḷikkumbōḷ
ennamma cārē aṇaññiṭēṇē
vāripuṇarnn-enne prēmattāl
kāruṇya-pīyūṣam ēkēṇam ammē

O my Mother, please come when I call out 'Amma, Amma!'. Please hug me and shower me with your purifying compassion, Mother!

onnum ariyātta piñcukuññallē ñān
kai piṭiccenne nayiccīṭaṇē
kai-viṭṭeṅgānum pōyāl
mōhakkaṭalil ñān vīzhum ammē

Am I not a tiny ignorant child? Please take my hand and lead me. If you let go of my hand and leave, I will fall into the ocean of delusion, O Mother.

tūmandahāsattin tēnmazhayāl
akatāril kuḷirēkīṭēṇē
kanivārnnorā kaṭākṣattāl
ānandāmṛtam-ēkēṇam ammē

Please soothe my mind with the cooling rain of your beautiful smile. Mother, with your sidelong glance, please bestow immortal bliss upon me.

mārōṭu cērttenne prēmattin toṭṭilil
āṭṭiyāṭṭi urakkēṇamē

śuddha-snēhattil-āzhttīṭaṇē
padatārilekk-enne cērkkēṇam ammē

Hold me close to you. Rock me to sleep in the cradle of your divine love. O Mother, immerse me in pure love and draw me close to your feet!

ammē ammē nitya (Malayalam)

ammē ammē nitya-svarūpamē
nirmala mānasa-mūrttē
ñān aṙiññīṭila nin mahā-vaibhavam
viśvam camaykkum poruḷē

O Mother! Your true form is eternal. Your shrine is the pure-heart. I cannot fathom your glories, O Supreme Essence, Creatrix of this universe!

uḷḷil-uṇḍendamma enna satyam
ñān aṙiyāyka vicitram
amma tan tēnmozhi muttukaḷ atrayum
satyam uṇarttiṭunnu ātma-bōdham teḷicciṭunnu

It is indeed strange that I do not know the Truth within me that is my Mother. Her sweet words awaken the knowledge of the Truth, and reveal the Self.

amma tan darśanam janma-puṇyam
ennu ninappū makkaḷ
cittam teḷiññ-uḷḷam śuddhamāy tīrukil
janmasāphalyam ākum karmadoṣam akannu
pōkum

To receive Her darshan is the blessing of this life. Her children know this is true. If our mind becomes light and pure, our life will be fulfilled and our karmic troubles will fade away.

ammē dēvi amṛtēśvarī (Malayalam)

ammē dēvi amṛtēśvarī
ennil nī bhakti ēkū dēvī

O Mother, eternal goddess, please give me devotion!

ammē dēvī paramēśvarī
ennil nī śakti ēkū dēvī

O Mother, supreme goddess, please grant me strength!

ammē dēvī jagadīśvarī
nin pāda padmattil cērkkukillē

O Mother, goddess of the world, will You not keep me close to Your feet?

ammē dēvī bhuvanēśvari
ennil nin vātsalyam ēkukillē

O Mother, goddess of the Earth, will You not bless me with Your affection?

ammē dēvī sarvēśvarī
ennil nin vidya ēkū dēvī

O Mother, goddess of all, please grant me Your knowledge.

ammē dēvi prāṇēśvarī
ennil nin kāruṇyam ēkū dēvī

O Mother, goddess of my life, please bestow Your compassion on me!

ammē dēvī māhēśvarī
ennil nin viśvāsam ēkukillē

O Mother, great goddess, will You not grant me faith in You?

ammē dēvī viśvēśvarī
ennil nin prēmam coriyukillē

O Mother, goddess of the Universe, will You not shower Your divine love on me?

ammē amṛtēśvarī, ammē bhuvanēśvarī
ammē jagadīśvarī, ammē sarvēśvarī

ammē dēvī snēha-svarūpiṇi (Malayalam)

ammē dēvī snēha-svarūpiṇi
makkaḷil nin kṛpa coriyēṇamē
āśrayamaruḷū abhayamaruḷū
ammē nin makkaḷe kāttiḍaṇē

O Mother Goddess, embodiment of love, please shower Your grace upon Your children! Grant us refuge, O Mother, and protect Your children.

ammē dēvi sarvēśvarī
aviḍutte darśanam ēkīḍaṇē
eviḍeyāṇammē nīyirippū en
hṛdayattilō atō kōvililō

O Mother Devi, goddess of all, please grant Your darshan. O Mother, where are you? Are you in my heart, or in the temple?

ammē dēvī mahāmāyē
mōhavum mamatayum akattīḍaṇē

prārtthanayālum japattinālum
makkaḷe ammayil cērttiḍaṇē

O Mother Devi, great Maya, please dispel delusion and attachment. Through prayers and japa, please merge Your children in You.

ammē hṛdayēśvarī (Malayalam)

ammē hṛdayēśvarī
ende ī janmam nin tirupādattil
arppicciṭunn-ivaḷ ammē
darśanam ēkān kaniyukillē
ī kuññu paitale veṭiyarutē

O Mother, Goddess of my heart, I offer my life at your sacred feet. Will you not be compassionate and grant me your vision? Please do not abandon your little child.

ammē ninnōmal kuññine
cāratt-aṇaykkān tāmasamō?
yōgya alleṅkilum nin munnil ettiya
ī jīvane nī cērttīṭanē

Mother, why do you delay to bring your darling child close to you? I may not be deserving, but please draw this soul close to you.

ammē nin malarvāṭiyil
oru pūmoṭṭu ñānammē
nin karasparśam koṇḍu viṭartti
ninnilēkk-enne nī cērttīṭumō?

O Mother, I am a bud in your flower garden. With the touch of your hand, will you not make me blossom and merge in You?

ammē nin kāruṇya-dhārayāl
ende ī janmam dhanyamākkū
alleṅkil nin kṛpāvarṣattināy
etrayum janmaṅgaḷ kāttirikkām

Mother, bless this life in the flow of your compassion. I will wait lifetimes for Your shower of grace.

ammē hṛdayēśvari (Malayalam)

ammē hṛdayēśvari jagadīśvarī jaganāyaki
bhuvanēśvarī tripurēśvarī kāruṇya pradāyini

O Mother, goddess of my heart, goddess of the world, leader of all, goddess of the Earth, goddess of the three cities, bestower of compassion!

aviḍutte tṛkkaram koṇḍu enne uyarttēṇam
tūmandahāsam pozhikkēṇamē

Please lift me up with Your sacred hands. Bless me with Your beautiful smile.

śvētāmbaradhāriṇi śyāmaḷa manōhari
ninnil layippikku jagadambikē

O dark goddess, enchanting all, dressed in white, please dissolve me in You, Mother of the world!

ahambhāva hāriṇi pāpavināśini
akatāril mālinyam akattīṭaṇē

You remove ego and destroy sin. Please remove the impurities within me.

kamala sulōcani jñānaprakāśini
aviḍutte dīpam teḷiyikkaṇē

Your beautiful eyes are like lotus flowers, and you shine with the light of knowledge. Please shine Your light on us!

ammē karuṇāmayi (Malayalam)

ammē karuṇāmayi
bhuvanēśvari en hṛdayēśvari

O Mother, embodiment of compassion, goddess of the world, goddess of my heart.

māyāsvarūpiṇi śrī vidyē
rājarājēśvari kaiviṭallē
śivāni sarvāṇi mahākāḷi
prēmasvarūpiṇi pāhimām

Divine illusion, goddess of knowledge, queen of the gods, please hold my hand! Protect me, O Shivani, goddess of all, great Kali, embodiment of divine love.

satyattinum dharmattinum vazhikāṭṭiṭu
ādiparāśakti ōm śakti
jagadīśvari en ponnammē
lōkattin ellā duḥkham māṫṫittaru

Please show me the way of Truth and dharma, primordial goddess, essence of Om, great Shakti! My dearest mother, goddess of the world, please put an end to all the suffering of the world!

mahāpāpa nāśini śrī rājarājēśvari
viśvāsam tannenne rakṣikkū

ānanda rūpiṇi mahāmāya
saccidānanda svarūpiṇi

O queen goddess, destroyer of sin, please grant me faith and protect me. You are bliss, the great illusion, the very embodiment of satchidananda (existence, consciousness and bliss).

ammē nin māyā (Malayalam)

ammē nin māyā marubhūvil
alakṣyamāyi alaññu ī paital
oru tuḷḷi amṛtināyi kēzhum ikuññinu
amṛtavarṣamāyi ni peytiṙaṅgille?

O Amma! I wander aimlessly in the desert of Your illusion. I cry out to You for a drop of life-giving nectar. Will You not hear the cries of your child and rain down as ambrosia?

marīcikayām vastuvin pinnāle
ōṭi taḷarnnu ñān ammē
entinennaṙiyāte ētinennaṙiyāte
nityē ninne ñān vismariccu

O Mother! I am tired, running after the mirage of vain desires. O eternal One! Not knowing why or for what, I failed to remember You.

sarvatilum nin uṇma darśikkuvān
ennenikkāvum endammē
paṙayu paṙayu jagadambikē
aṙivin poruḷē hṛdayāmbikē
kanivin poruḷē kamalāmbikē

O Mother! When will I see your existence in everything? Tell me, tell me, O Mother! You are Knowledge, and the queen of my heart. You are compassion, the Mother dwelling in the lotus of my heart!

ammē nin rūpam (Malayalam)

ammē nin rūpam kāṇān kotikkunnu
ammē nin nādam kēḷkkān kotikkunnu
ammē nin sparśam ariyān kotikkunnu
ammē nin mandahāsam nukarān kotikkunnu

Mother I long to see Your form, I long to hear Your voice. I long to know Your touch, I long to sip the sweetness of Your smile.

tṛkkaram koṇḍenne ūṭṭān varillē
picca naḍakkumbōḷoppam varille
kāruṇya pīyuṣām nukaruvān innende
cārattu vannu nī aṇayukillē ammē
cārattu vannu nī aṇayukillē

Will You not come and feed me with Your sacred hand? Will You not walk beside my toddling steps? Will you not come today, that I may drink the nectar of your compassion?

aṇayumbōzhenne nī vātsalya-pūrvamā
mārōḍu cērttu nī ōmanikkillē
svapnamāy... pinne satyamāy bhavikkumī
padamalaraḍikaḷil abhayam ēkillē
ā pādapatmattil nī cērkkukillē

Coming close, will You not hug me and shower me with affection? This may happen in a dream and then become Truth. Will You not grant me refuge at Your lotus feet? Will You not unite me to those lotus feet?

ammē ammē ammē ammē
padamalaraḍikaḷil abhayam ēkillē
ā pādapatmattil nī cērkkukillē

O Mother, will You not grant me refuge at Your lotus feet? Please unite me to your lotus feet?

ammē parāśaktī (Malayalam)

ammē parāśaktī dēvī – en
manassil irunnenne nayikkū

O Mother Devi, Parashakti, lead me and dwell in my heart!

āśrayam nīyē ammē – en
karmaṅgaḷ nirmalamākkū
inn-enikk-ēkumō ammē
ninnil uracca bhakti

Mother, You are my refuge. Please make my actions pure. Please grant me perfect devotion to You today?

nityānandamē ammē
nī allāt-ārumill-abhayam
ennē muruke piḍikkū ammē
nanmayilēkku naṭattu

O Mother, eternal bliss, You are my only refuge. Mother, please hold me tight, and make me tread the path of goodness.

añjani putra (Malayalam)

añjani putra kēsari nandana
hanumanta en priya nāthā
kāñcana dēha ratna kuṇḍala
hanumanta en priya nāthā

O son of Anjana and Kesari, O Hanuman, my dear Lord! Your body is golden and you wear jewelled earrings. O Hanuman, my beloved Lord!

jñāna-svarūpa guṇaśīla
balam buddhi vidya nalkēṇamē
nī en mana kapiyin īśan
hanumanta en priya nāthā

Embodiment of knowledge, you possess all the divine qualities. Please grant me strength, intelligence and wisdom! You are the Lord of my monkey mind, O Hanuman, my dear Lord!

jay jay māruti mahāvīrā... hōy
jay jay māruti mahādhīrā
nin nāmam en priya nāmam

Victory to the great heroic one, son of the wind god! Victory to the great courageous one, son of the wind god! Your name is dear to my heart.

śrīrāma bhakta śrīrāma dūta
śrīrāma pādattil cērkkēṇamē
nin nāthan en priya nāthan
śrīrām jay rām jay jay rām

Devotee of Lord Rama, messenger of Sri Rama! Please bring me to Lord Rama's feet. Your Lord is my beloved Lord. O victory to Lord Rama!

jay śrīrām jay hanumān
jay śrīrām jay hanumān

Victory to Lord Rama! victory to Hanuman!

Antakaa Ammalle (Finnish)

Antakaa Ammalle surujen taakka
Hänellä on voimaa kantaa.
Rakkaus teissä jo on
Ei sitä voi kukaan antaa

Give the burden of your sorrows to Amma. She has the strength to bear it. Love is already within you. No one can give it to you.

Amma siunaa meitä sydämellä
hyvällä ja jalolla
Pimeyden voi vain voittaa
Rakkauden rakkauden rakkauden valolla!

Amma, bless us with a good and kind heart. Only the light of love can overcome darkness!

Etsikää onnea ikuista
Maailmasta sitä ei saa
Hakekaa aitoa rakkautta
Sydämen se puhdistaa.

Seek eternal happiness. The world cannot give it to you. Look for that inner true love that will purify your heart.

Menkää syvälle sisimpään,
Amma siellä odottaa teitä

Ottaa syliinsä lämpimään
Hellästi halailee meitä

Go deep within your heart where Amma is waiting. She takes us in Her warm embrace and caresses us tenderly.

avanavanār-enn (Malayalam)

avan avan ār-enn-ariyāykilō
ariyunnat-ellām-inn-anyam ākum
ariyunnat-ākilō svātma-bhāvam
anyamāy onnum-illennu kāṇum

If we do not know who we really are, all the knowledge we accumulate is vain. When we are established in our true Self, we will realize that nothing is separate from us.

arivillānilayil nām ārumāyum
avivēkiyāy ninn-aṭikūṭiṭum
ñān ennum nī ennum nammaḷ ennum
colli kalahiccu madamēttiṭum

As long as we are ignorant of our true Self, we will stand and fight with others. Full of pride and arrogance, we will fight over 'me', 'you' and 'us'.

aham ennat-ātmāvin sphuraṇam ennu
amaratva-bōdhikaḷ uṇarttiṭunnu
aham enna tattvatte anubhūtiyil
avabōdhiccāl janmam saphalamallō

The immortal ones tell us the individual self is a spark of the supreme Self. Our life is fulfilled when we gain insight into this Self-principle and bring it into the realm of our experience.

Awlaadi, awlaadi (Arabic)

Awlaadi, Awlaadi, Ahibaa'i
Laa tahzanuu, laa tay'asuu
Awlaadi, Awlaadi, Ahibaa'i
Ifrahuu, ghannuu, wab'tasimuu

My children, my children, my dear ones, don't be sad, don't lose hope. My children, my children, my dear ones, be happy! Sing, and smile!

Al Hayatuu fiiha afrahun... wa fiiha aydan atraahun
La tajaluu al atraaha... tulghi jamalal afraaha

Life has happy moments and also sad moments. Don't let the sad moments steal the beauty of the happy ones.

Laa tansau.... farahal atfaali
Abqu fiikumu.... bara'atal atfaali

Remember the happiness of children and keep childlike innocence in you.

Awlaadi, Awlaadi, Laa tahzanuu
Ifrahuu, ghannuu, wab'tasimuu...

My children, my children, don't be sad. Be happy, sing, and smile!

Ahibbu baadakum, ahibbul' hayata
Ahibbut' tabiiata, ahibbun' nabaata
Ahibbut' tuyuura, ahibbuz' zuhuura
ahibbuch' chammsa, ahibbul' qamara

Love one another, love life, love nature. Love the plants, love the birds, love the flowers, love the Sun, love the Moon.

Ahibbu kulla ma… min hawlikum
Abibbu kulla men… huwa hawlakum

Love everything around you, love everything around you.

Sallu lillaahi… tawakkalu a'layyhi
Sallu lillaahi… tawajjahu ilay'hi

Pray to God. Trust God. Pray to God. Move towards Him.

āyiram kātuḷḷa kāḷi (Malayalam)

āyiram kātuḷḷa kāḷiyammē – ī
arivillā paitalin mozhikaḷ nī kēlkunnuvō

Mother Kali with a thousand ears, do You hear your ignorant child's words?

āyiram kāṇṇuḷḷa kāḷiyammē – ī
arivillā paitalin karmaṅgaḷ kāṇunnuvō

Mother Kali with a thousand eyes, do You see your ignorant child's actions?

āyiram kātuḷḷa kāḷiyammē
āyiram kaṇṇuḷḷa kāḷiyammē

O Mother Kali with a thousand ears, Mother Kali with a thousand eyes!

sarvatum ariyunna kāḷiyammē
ñān māyayām svapnattil mayaṅgīṭunnu

All-knowing Mother Kali, I am asleep in this illusory dream of Maya.

nin snēha vātsalya tiramālakāḷ puṇarumbōḷ
ñān vīṇḍum uṇarnnīḍunnu

When the waves of Your affection enfold me, I awaken again.

en vākku nin vākku ākēṇamē
en karmam nin karmam āvēṇamē
en iccha nin iccha ākkēṇamē
en vazhi ninnilēkk-ettēṇamē

May Your words be my words, may Your actions be my actions. May Your will be my will. May my path bring me to You.

ennile ninne ñān ariyēṇamē

May I know You within me.

jay jay mā... jay jay mā... jay jay mā...
jay jay mā... jay jay mā... kāḷi mā...

bārō bārō bālagōpāla (Kannada)

bārō bārō bālagōpāla
tuḷasi mālanē bārō
bārō bārō bālagōpāla
tuḷasimālanē bārō

Come little Krishna, adorned with a Tulasi garland. Come!

tāyi yaśodeya kandanu nīnu
nandagōpana kaṇmaṇi nīnu
vṛndāvana vihārī kṛṣṇā
rādhāramaṇā śrīkṛṣṇā

You are the darling of Mother Yashoda, the beloved child of Nanda. O Krishna, who moves about Vrindavan! O Krishna, the Lord of Radha!

gollara maneyā bēṇṇē kaddē
gōpijanara manava kaddē
vēṇuvilōlā śrīkṛṣṇā
vēdānta sārā śrīkṛṣṇā

You stole butter from the homes of the cowherds and you stole their hearts. O Krishna, who rejoices in playing the flute! O Krishna, the essence of the Vedas!

bālagōpālā (vēṇūgōpālā)
gōparipālā (gōpijanalōlā)
muraḷīlōlā (bhaktaparipālā)
vṛndāvana bālā (gōpālā)
gōvindā harī gōpālāj

bhagavan ham par (Hindi)

bhagavan ham par dayā karō
bhagavan ham par dayā karō

O God, have mercy on us!

jīv sabhī hai bālak tērē
dukh vipdāō me he ghērē
tum hī sab kē rakṣak svāmī
sab kī pīḍā harō
ham par dayā karō

All beings are Your children. Sorrows and calamities surround them. You alone are the protector of all, O Lord. Remove our sufferings, have mercy on us!

man kō jitne bhōg lagāyē
pyās hamārī baḍtī jāyē
maruthal he ham bin nehā kē
ban kar mēgh jharō
ham par dayā karō

The more we feed our minds with material pleasures, the more our thirst increases. We are like a desert without rain. Please pour down on us as a divine rain. Have mercy on us!

rūp dikhāvō tum jan jan mēṅ
jōt jalāvō tum kaṇ kaṇ mēṅ
apnē sē up jī jagtī mēṅ
apnā āp bharō
ham par dayā karō

Show us Your beautiful form in each and every being. Shine Your pure light in each and every cell and atom. Let Your all-pervading Self fill this world. Have mercy on us!

bhajeham gaṇēśam (Sanskrit)

bhajeham gaṇēśam viriñcādi vandyam
prapañcasya sāram punītam vinītaḥ
suśānta svabhāvam śubham bhūrimōdam
vibhum viśvadēvam prabhum susmitāsyam

We sing to Ganesha who is worshipped by Brahma and other gods. The pure, humble One is the energy of the universe. The One of calm nature, auspicious and abundant with joy, the mighty Lord of the universe with a sweet smile!

śivam jñāna-dantam param śrī vahantam
umāṅkē lasantam bṛhad-dehavantam
mahānāda-rūpam budhair-nitya-sēvyam
mahādēva-tējōbhavam dēvamīḍē

The child of Shiva and Shakti, whose tusks symbolize wisdom, He who is a part of Uma (Parvati). One with a mighty body, the embodiment of the primordial sound Om. Ever served by the wise, He contains the brilliant splendor of Shiva and is praised by the devas.

pracaṇḍam pravarṣam prabhāpūrṇa gātram
pramattam prasannam pratarkkairagamyam
dhruvam dhūmra-varṇam calachūrppa-karṇṇam
avarṇṇam supūrṇam gaṇēśam bhajēham

The great One with the effulgent body, the One intoxicated with the knowledge of the Supreme. Blissful One, unattainable through conjecture. Eternal One of dark hue, with large elephant ears, the indescribable, complete One.

satām mānacōram bhavāmbōdhi-pāram
sthiram cārurūpam priyam sarva-mūlam
sadā svaprakāśam virūpākṣam-īśam
jagad-dēśikam śrī gaṇēśam bhajeham

You steal the hearts of devotees and take them across the ocean of worldly existence, O unchanging One of beautiful form! Beloved and the root of everything, ever Self-effulgent emanation of the Supreme Consciousness (Shiva). We worship Ganesha, the Lord of the Universe.

namaḥ śubhra-kīrtē jagajjanma dātrē
paritrāhi mām sarva-sandāna-mūrtē
namaḥ śārṅgiṇē cakrapāṇē namastē
namaḥ śūlinē pāśinē bhō namastē

Salutations to the splendid One who witnesses the birth of the Universe. Help us, O healer of all! Salutations again and again to the wielder of the bow and discus. Salutations again and again to the One holding the trident.

bhayamannadi (Telugu)

bhayamannadi antaraṅga
pariṇāmamu kādā
dēhādulu dīni kāraṇamā lēka
nēnu nādanubhāva prēritamā

Is fear only a mental modification? Are body and worldly objects the cause of fear; or is it the feeling that 'I am the body' and 'the objects are mine'?

dhanikunaku cōra bhayam
bhōgiki rōga bhayam
adhikāriki cyuti bhayam
jīvulaku maraṇa bhayam

The rich fear thieves stealing their property. The self-indulgent fear disease. The powerful fear downfall; and all living beings fear death.

vīṭi mūlam ajñānam
āśrayiñcu guru pādam

The root cause for all fear is ignorance of our true Self. The remedy is to take refuge at the feet of the Guru.

amma cūpu jñāna mārgam
ācariñcu śravaṇa mananam
anātma nirākaraṇam
sadvastu niścayam

Amma will show the path of knowledge. Start listening, and contemplate on Guru's teachings. With firm conviction in that one Truth, discard all that is not it.

reṇḍavadi lēdanu abhayam
ēkam-ēvādvitīyam
guruśāstra upadēśam
okaṭē mārgamu

Fearlessness is only that understanding that there is nothing second to the Self. The only way to understand this Truth is through scripture, the teachings of the Guru.

bhītiyilāyen manam (Malayalam)

bhītiyilāyen manam innōṭunna
paikiṭāv-ennapōl kēṇiṭunnu
vātsalya pāl curattunn-oru payyupōl
enneyum vāri puṇarukillē

My mind is crying out in fear like a new-born calf. O Mother, you give the milk of tender affection. Will You not embrace me?

anyamāy māṙunna ī dharma-pātayil
ārōrumillāte ēkanāy ñān
munnōṭṭu pōkuvān bhayamuṇḍat-eṅkilum
ammatan makanalle pōyiṭum ñān
pōyiṭum ñān

On the path of dharma, I feel alienated and alone, with no one by my side. I am afraid to go ahead, but I am Amma's child. I will move forward!

ñān ūtum vēṇuvin nādaṅgaḷ okkeyum
ammatan snēhattin īṇamallē
kusṛtikaḷ kāṭṭumbōḷ okkeyum ciri tūkum
ambike kaniyēṇē kṛpayālē nī
kṛpayālē nī

All the melodies flowing from my flute are set to the tune of Amma's love. O Ambika! You smile at my mischief. Please shower your grace upon me!

samsāra-lōkamām uṙalilāy bandhiyām
enne nī mōcitan ākkukillē
prēmamām tūveṇṇa kaṭṭutinnunn-avan
eṅkilum ōmana kaṇṇanallē
kaṇṇanallē

I am bound by the mortar of this worldly existence. Will you not free me? Even though I may steal and eat the fresh butter of your love, am I not still your dear little Krishna?

Celebramos la vida (Spanish)

Celebramos la vida
La madre divina está aquí
por mi, por ti

Let us celebrate life. The divine mother is here for me and for you.

Jay mā... jay mā... jay mā... jay mā...
Si nos llegan problemas,
la madre enseña como brillar, poder volar

If problems come, Mother will teach us how to shine, how to fly.

Nos llena de gracia
y nunca descansa abrazar
Amar no puede parar

She fills us with grace, and never tires of hugging. She never stops loving.

La vida entera la madre espera
entregar adorar
Nos quiere salvar

Mother is waiting for us to surrender our lives to love. She wants to save us.

cilambōli kēṭṭuvō (Malayalam)

cilambōli kēṭṭuvō ñān – kaṇṇande
vēṇuvin nādavum kēṭṭō
gadgadakaṇṭhanāy ēreyalaññu
kārmukil varṇṇane tēḍi

Did I hear the sound of anklets? Did I hear the sound of Kannan's flute? Choked with emotion, I have been wandering all over, searching for the One with the complexion of rain clouds.

ēkanāy nilkkum kadambamē nīyumā
kaṇṇane kāttirikkunnō
yamunā puḷinavum maunam ārnnatu
kaṇṇan varāññatinālō

O solitary kadamba tree, do you also wait for Kannan? Such silence surrounds the banks of the Yamuna river. Is it because Kannan hasn't come?

kaṇṇā... kaṇṇā... kaṇṇā... kaṇṇā...
pūnilāvoḷi tūki nilkkunna paurṇami
tinkaḷum mḷānamāy nilppatentē
varikayillē ā kāyāmbūvarṇṇan
aṇayukillē ā prēmarūpan?

Why does the full moon, spilling gentle moonlight, seem despondent? Won't the dark-complexioned One come? Won't that embodiment of love come close?

Cógeme la mano (Spanish)

Cógeme la mano
Ponme en tu regazo
Llévame Contigo
Soltando mis deseos
Fundida en tu Luz

Hold my hand, put me in Your lap. Take me with You. Free me of my desires and merge me in Your light.

Enséñame a reír
de corazón
Sonriendo desde Ti
Sonriendo desde Ti

Teach me to laugh from my heart, smiling from You (God's essence).

Enséñame a amar
sin esperar
Sirviéndole al Amor
Sirviéndole al Amor

Teach me to love without expectations, serving love (in everyone).

Enséñame a ser
quien yo soy
Reflejo de tu Verdad
Reflejo de tu Verdad

Teach me to be who I truly am, a reflection of Your Truth.

Cuando la madre tierra (Spanish)

Cuando la Madre Tierra está gritando de dolor
y el humano ha perdido toda su conexión
Imagina flores blancas cayendo a tu alrededor
en los mares, las montañas y en toda la creación.

When Mother Earth is screaming in pain, and humans have lost all inner connection, imagine white flowers falling around you, in the seas, the mountains and in all creation.

Lokah Samastah Sukhino Bhavantu
Lokah Samastah Sukhino Bhavantu

May all beings in all the worlds be happy!

La avaricia, la ignorancia nos llevaron hasta aquí,
Madre Tierra, Pachamama te pedimos tu perdón.
Imagina que estas lleno de una luz pura de amor
que la expandes al planeta, siente la sanación.

Greed and ignorance brought us here. Mother Earth, Pachamama (another name for Mother Earth), we beg your forgiveness! Imagine that you are filled with the pure light of love, that you expand to the planet. Feel the healing.

Si te sientes oprimido o con vacío interior
Recuerda que no estás sólo, Amma está en tu corazón
Cada célula de tu cuerpo comienza a brillar
Desde pies hasta cabeza siente todo iluminar

If you feel oppressed by inner emptiness, remember that you are not alone. Amma is in your heart. Every cell of your body brightens and from feet to head, feel completely illuminated.

Pachamama, Madre Tierra, por favor perdónanos
Pachamama, Madre Tierra, te pedimos tu perdón

Pachamama, Mother Earth, please forgive us. Pachamama, Mother Earth, we beg for your forgiveness.

ḍamaruka-nātha (Sanskrit)

ḍamaruka-nātha śivane
bhōlēnātha śivane
kāśīnātha śivane
ōm namaḥ śivāya ōm namaḥ śivāya

nīlakaṇṭhā śivane
pārvatīśā śivane
nandikēśa śivane
ōm namaḥ śivāya ōm namaḥ śivāya

ōm namaḥ śivāya ōm namaḥ śivāya
ōm mahādēvāya mahārūpāya mahākālāya śivane

ōm namaḥ śivāya ōm namaḥ śivāya
ōm namaḥ śivāya ōm namaḥ śivāya

ōm harāya namaḥ ōm śivāya namaḥ
ōm balāya namaḥ ōm kālāya namaḥ

Devi awaken your children (English)

Devi Devi! awaken your children, hear our prayer.
Devi Devi! we will come running, hearing you call.

We hear you calling, in our heart,
to love and serve with compassion,
to go beyond greed and pride.
Make earth a heaven for everyone.
Make earth a heaven for everyone.

Laugh from the heart, healing all wounds.
Chase away the darkness deep within.
Devi is right here, don't waste time,
Keep your focus on the goal.
Keep your focus on the goal.

dēvi mahāśaktī (Malayalam)

dēvi mahāśaktī māyē manōmayi
ambikē dēvi kāḷi mahēśvari
nin kṛpa ennil ennum uṇḍākēṇamē

O Devi, great goddess, divine illusion, Mother Kali, great goddess! May Your grace be with me always.

ammē jaganmayi akhilāṇḍēśvari
ānandamāyi dēvi mahēśvari

O Mother, you pervade the world, goddess of the universe, embodiment of bliss, O Devi, great goddess!

śāradē durgē ambā mahēśvari
ambā jagadambā dēvi mahēśvari

Mother Saraswati, Durga, great goddess, Devi...

īśvarī ambē ātmasvarūpiṇi dēvi
ambā... ambā... ambā...

O Goddess, Mother, the true Self, Devi, Mother...

dēvi mātē durgē (Malayalam)

dēvi mātē durgē mātē kāḷi mātē jaganmātē
dēvi mātē durgē mātē kāḷi mātē jaganmātē
viśva mātē lōkamātē śakti mātē gauri mātē
vēda mātē yōga mātē jñāna mātē sarva mātē

lakṣmi mātē gauri mātē mahāmāyē śāradāmbē
pāhi pāhi sadā dēvi dēhi dēhi sadā kṛpām

O mother Lakshmi, mother Gauri, divine illusion, mother Saraswati! Please protect me always, O Devi, and always bestow your grace!

vidya tannu nī kaniyu śakti nalku bhakti nalku
satyaniṣṭhar-ākku dēvi dharmam ēki mukti nalku

Be compassionate, O mother, and grant us knowledge. Give us strength, give us devotion! Devi, make us steadfast in Truth, and grant us knowledge of dharma. Lead us to liberation!

jay jay mā jay jay mā jay jay mā jay jay mā
jay jay mā jay jay mā jay jay mā jay jay mā

dīnabandhō (Sanskrit)

dīnabandhō karuṇasindhō
pāhi mām tava pāda namastē

O Krishna, friend of the distressed, ocean of compassion! Protect me. I worship your lotus feet.

kaḷakaḷanādinī-yamunānikuñjē
madhuram madhuram vādatimuraḷi
mōhanam mōhanam tava śubharūpam
vasatu mama hṛdi satatam satatam

I hear the melody of your flute in the groves of *tulasi* growing on the banks of the merrily flowing Yamuna. Let your beautiful and auspicious form illumine my heart.

dhimidhimi-dhimidhimi nṛtyati madhuripu
dṛśyam anupamam rāsa nṛtyōtsavam
janma-vināśanam pāpavimōcanam
lasatu mama hṛdi satatam satatam

As you dance the *rasalila*, your movements enthrall me. The sight of you destroys my sin and saves me from further births. Please dance in my heart forever!

jaya jaya kṛṣṇa jaya śrī kṛṣṇa

Du er mit smukke hjem (Danish)

Du er mit smukke hjem, Moder Jord
Al min næring får jeg fra dig Moder Jord
Tak Moder Jord

You are my beautiful home, Mother Earth. All nourishment comes from you, Mother Earth. Thank you, Mother Earth!

Hvor skal jeg leve hvis ikke i dig?
Hvor skal jeg lære hvis ikke i dig?
Tak Moder Jord

Where will I live if not in You? Where will I learn if not in You? Thank you Mother Earth!

Vi skal beskytte dig Moder Jord
Ikke udnytte dig Moder Jord
Tak Moder Jord

We must protect you, Mother Earth, not exploit you. Thank you, Mother Earth!

jai ma, jai jai ma, jai jai jai ma
jai ma, jai jai ma, jai jai jai ma
jai jai jai ma

ēk ēk jap sē (Hindi)

ēk ēk jap sē jīvan bitāyā
rām bhakt hanumān
ō rām bhakt hanumān

O Hanuman, devotee of Lord Ram! Your entire life was spanned by each chant of your beloved Ram's name!

jay bajraṅgi hamumān
rām rām bōlō rām

Victory to mighty Hanuman! Chant Ram Ram Ram!

baccōṅ kō tū pyārā lāgē
rāmjī kā tū sabsē pyārā
mahāvīr hanumān
ō mahāvīr hanumān

Children find you adorable. You are the favorite of Ram. O great brave Hanuman!

rām-dūt ban pahuṅce laṅkā
sītā maiyā kō diyā sandēśā
rām-dūt hanumān
ō rām-dūt hanumān

Becoming the messenger of Ram, you reached Lanka and delivered the Lord's message to Mother Sita. O Hanuman, messenger of Ram!

eḷimayānavaḷ (Tamil)

eḷimayānavaḷ ammā inimayānavaḷ
anpukoṇḍu makkaḷai aravaṇaippavaḷ
śāntamānavaḷ ammā śaktiyānavaḷ
tunpam nīkkiyē ennai kākkum annayē

O Mother, You are the embodiment of simplicity and sweetness. With motherly love You embrace all. Your very nature is peace and divine strength. You protect me and remove all my sorrows.

karuṇayānavaḷ ammā kāḷiyānavaḷ
kaṇṇanāki makkaḷai kavarntizhuppavaḷ
annaiyānavaḷ ammā tantaiyānavaḷ
akantai nīkkiyē enai uyarttum annayē

O Mother, You are truly Kali, filled with boundless compassion. You steal the hearts of people by assuming Krishna bhava. O Mother, You are the divine mother and father of this Universe. You remove my ego and uplift me.

pūrṇamānavaḷ ammā putirumānavaḷ
guruvumāki makkaḷai karai sērppavaḷ
tōzhiyānavaḷ ammā tōṇiyānavaḷ
paṫṫru nīkkiyē tannil sērkkum annayē

O Mother, You are the perfection that is a mystery. You are the Guru, who takes all your children safely across this ocean of samsara. O Mother, You are friend and rescuer of all. Remove our attachments and merge us into Yourself.

śaraṇam śaraṇam śaraṇam amṛtēśvari
śaraṇam śaraṇam śaraṇam jagadīśvari

O immortal goddess, goddess of the world, grant us refuge!

Em habria ahava (Hebrew)

em habria ahava tehora
ima kali sheli ima kali sheli

Mother of creation, of pure love, my mother, Kali!

karvi oti elaich
leolam al taazvi et yadi

ba lev ima kali rikdi
shiri mizmor atik ve sodi

Bring me close to You. Never let go of my hand. Mother Kali, dance in my heart. Sing your ancient secret chant!

betfila amuka etmaser
ve al I emet avater
bli retzonot mishel atzmi
she tishaer esh ahavati

In deep prayer, I'll surrender, I'll let go of untruth. May the fire of my love free me of my desires.

Engulfed in this dark world (English)

Engulfed in this dark world of fear,
Amma surely sees my tears.
Though we may be miles apart,
Amma always knows my heart.

I long for your form.
I long for your form.
I long for your form before my eyes.
I long for your form before my eyes.

Like the rainbow after a storm,
Bless me with your sacred form.
Hold my hand through this night.
Guide me to eternal light.

Immersed in gems of memories,
Reveal Yourself inside of me.
Love is the path,
Truth is the light,
May the flame of faith burn bright.

ma jai ma jai ma jai ma
ma jai ja jai ma jai ma

en manaceppil (Malayalam)

en manaceppil ennennum nī oru
niṙamōlum mayilppīli āyirunnu
ōrō uṣassilum sandhyayilum nin
mōhana varṇṇaṅgaḷ nī niṙaccu

You were always a colorful peacock feather, safe in the jewel-chest of my heart. At every dawn and dusk, You filled my heart with enchanting colors.

nin varṇṇa rājikaḷ ōrttōrttu ñān ennum
ninnōṭ aṭukkān koticcuvallō
ā niṙakāntiyil ñān aliññīṭavē
śōkaṅgaḷ okke maṙannuvennō

Constantly remembering those bewitching colors, I longed to come closer to you. As I merged into your lucid beauty, I forgot all my sorrow.

nin divyarūpam en hṛttil teḷiyumbōḷ
aṙiyāten nayanam tuḷumbunnuvō
janmāntaraṅgaḷāy mōhanarūpam en
uḷḷattil ennum niṙaññirunnu

As your divine form fills my heart, unknowingly my eyes overflow with tears. Your lovely form has filled my heart in all my previous lives.

enne nayikkuvān (Malayalam)

enne nayikkuvān nī vēṇam ammē
kaiviṭalle pāzhil nīyennē
ariññill ulakil onnumē bhadramāy
nin karāślēṣattin oppamāyētume

Mother! please lead me. If you let go of my hand, my life will be barren. I know that nothing in this world can make me as secure as your loving embrace.

uṭayārnna vigraham vārkkunna nērattā
daṇḍanam santatam lōkārttham-ākavē
tyajiccīṭ-arutē ī vazhi tārayil
nin pāda-mudrakaḷ paticcorī hṛdayam

When the vigraha (image) is being sculpted, the chiseling makes it perfect for the world. My heart bears the imprint of your divine feet. Do not abandon me by the wayside.

ninnil ninn-akalunnatin vyatha ammē
sahiyuvān-āvillen hṛttil enn-ariyuka
nirddayam nī maṙannīṭilum piriyilla
(amma nī enne maṙannālum piriyilla)
ariyām-itokke parīkṣaṇaṅgaḷ

O Mother! I cannot bear the pain of separation from you; but, if you have no compassion and forget me, I will accept it as your test of my faith and still cling to you.

ennu kēḷkkum (Malayalam)

ennu kēḷkkum nin svaram-ennuḷḷil
kātōrtt-irippū kaṇṇā nin tōzhī
kātōrtt-irippū kaṇṇā
oru naṙu pīli ñān ninakku tannu
tirumuṭi azhakil cūṭīṭumō

When will I hear your song within me, O Kanna, my friend? I wait eagerly. I gave you a colorful peacock feather. Won't you wear it in your dark hair?

maṫṫoru gōpiyē nōkkiyālum
ennōṭ-ennapōl-ennu tōnnum
en manassin śruti-tāḷavum nī
teṫṫāte vēṇuvil cērttīṭaṇē

Even when you look at another Gopi, within me I will believe that you are seeing me. You are the music in my heart. Please play me as the melody of your flute.

mādhuryam ōlunna mādhavā en manam
nin pādam patiyum yamunayākkū
ennude hṛdaya kallōlaṅgaḷe
nin prēmagaṅgayil cērttīṭaṇē

O Madhava, my sweet Lord! Make my heart the Yamuna which bathes your feet. Please merge the small wavelets of my heart in the river of your love.

entinō vēṇḍi (Malayalam)

entinō vēṇḍippiṭaññu nirantaram
āreyō tēṭittiraññu
māṙum prapañcattil māṙāttat-onnine
kāṇāte ñānum alaññu

My heart ached in longing as I searched. I wandered this transient world without finding the changeless Truth.

amma tan mōhanarūpam kāṇke
ennuḷḷil dīpam teḷiññu
māṫṫamillāttoru satyavastu amma
tānenna bōdham teḷiññu

When I saw Amma's radiant form, my heart lit up in joy. I knew that Amma was eternal, the changeless reality.

eṅkilum ende ā śīlam innu
tāne svabhāvamāy tīrnnu
ammaye viṭṭu ñān vīṇḍum prapañcatte
vārippuṇarnnu taḷarnnu

Yet, my habits are entrenched in me. They have become my character. As I leave Amma and again embrace the world, I become lost and exhausted.

ammē ī jīvitam dussahamāy tiṅgum
vāsana tīrtta mōhattāl
onneniykkāśrayam ēkū nī endeyī
muḷvazhi tannil tuṇaykkū

O Mother! This life seems unbearable. My desires were created by my tendencies. Won't you comfort and guide me as I walk this thorny path?

cintakaḷ nīkkitteḷikkū uḷḷil
amma tan rūpam niṙaykkū
ammaye mātram ninaykkuvān ennumen
mānasam nirmalamākkū

Remove my thoughts and enlighten me. May your enthralling form fill my heart. Make my heart pure so that I remember only you, Mother.

ammayennuḷḷil uṇarū ende
uḷḷile bōdham uṇarttū
ōrō cuvaṭilum tāṅgum taṇalumāy
nī tanne ennum nayikkū

O Mother! Awaken within me. Awaken as the pure consciousness within me. Guide each step of mine forever. You are my shade and support.

entu colvān-uddhavare (Malayalam)

entu colvān-uddhavare ñaṅgaḷ-innu
vāsudeva vākyam-entenn-ōtuka cemmē
gōpikaḷ tan karaḷ kaṭṭu vrajatteyum viṭṭu pōyōn
yādavarkku rājanāyi vāzhukayallō

O Uddhava! What can we say? What message did Vasudeva send for us? He who stole the hearts of the gopis and left Vrindavan now reigns as the King of the Yadavas.

cōravṛtti ceyt-avarkku rāja-yōgam-ennō
atu kōriyiṭṭa brahma-dēvan nītimān-ennō
kalturuṅkil janiccavan tiriccaṅgu pōkān
kalpanayē ceytīḍuvān ārumillennō?

Is it possible for a thief to become a king? Is Brahma, who wrote such a destiny for Krishna, just? Is there no one to order the one born in a dungeon to return there?

gōpikanām antaraṅgē kārāgṛham nalkān
gōpabālan ceyta kuttam matiyāyiṭum
kalpakālam kazhivōḷam kiṭakkaṭṭe kaṇṇan
ghaṭattinkaḷ akapeṭṭa iḍam ennapōl

The wrongs committed by the cowherd boy are enough to sentence him to the prison of the gopis' hearts. Let him remain there till the end of time, like the blue sky enclosed in a pot.

bāhyanāya nandasūnu viśvāsyanalla avan
cāruvākyamōti nammē mōhitar-ākkum
antasthanāy māriyālō manaḥkkōvil nāthanavan
cintakaḷkkum sākṣiyāyi varttikkumallō

The external form of the son of Nanda cannot be trusted. He will delude us with sweet and loving words. If he dwells within us, however, he remains forever, the Lord of the temple of our hearts. He remains forever a witness to our thoughts.

Epsahna stin nihta (Greek)

Epsahna stin nihta mou Esena
Na yemiso tin zoii
Na hii ena noiima yia mena
Oli afti I prosmoni.

I looked for you in the night, to fill the gap in my life, that I might find a purpose for all these years of longing.

Kirthes to proii me ton agera
K' anastenaksi kardia
Soupa me lahtara kalimera
Ke me pires agalia

You came in the morning with the wind, and my heart sighed. With longing, I said, 'Welcome Mother,' and you took me in your arms.

Ela Amma ela Amma
Ela Amma stin kardia mas
Ela Amma ela Amma
Mine ki glikia Thea mas

Come Amma, come Amma, come Amma to our hearts. Come Amma, come Amma and stay there, our sweet Goddess

Ela Amma ela Amma
Ela Amma stin kardia mas
Ela Amma ela Amma
Mono si mas fernis tin hara

Come Amma, come Amma, come Amma to our hearts. Come Amma, come Amma, only You can bring us joy.

Ida mes sta matia sou Mitera
Ola t'astra ksafnika
Hilious ilious ke margaritaria
Na fotizoun ton dounia

Mother, suddenly I saw all the stars in Your eyes. Thousands of suns and pearls illumined the whole universe.

K'eyina mikro pedi diko sou
Me athoa tin kardia
Irthe i siyi mesa sto nou mou
Ke irini stin kardia.

And I became your little child with an innocent heart. My mind fell silent and I felt peace.

Ela Amma ela Amma
Ela Amma stin kardia mas
Ela Amma Ela Amma
Mine ki glikia Thea mas

Come Amma, come Amma, come Amma to our hearts. Come Amma, come Amma, and stay there, our sweet Goddess.

Ela Amma ela Amma
Ela Amma stin kardia mas
Ela Amma ela Amma
Na girisi pali i Athina

Come Amma, come Amma, come Amma to our hearts! Come Amma, come Amma, so that Athena (Goddess of Wisdom) returns again to our land!

Gotts himmel (German)

Gotts Himmel schimmert Azur
Mutter Ganga fühlt sich pur

God's azure skies shimmer, Mother Ganga feels pure.

Schwäne und Delfine glücklich schwimmen in Flüssen
O Mensch sitzt im Haus
betet zu Gottes Füssen

Swans and dolphins swim joyfully in the rivers. O man, sit in the house and pray for God's grace.

O Devi, Bhumi Devi,
Pacha Mama, Madre tierra,
Terre mere, Mutter Erde
Mother Earth, Madre Terra

Amma nimm die Egosucht
sie zerstört mit Wucht

Amma remove our ego. It destroys fiercely.

Beten zu Dir mit offnem Herz
oh Amma
Beten zu Dir mit offnem Herz
Nimm unseren Schmerz

We pray to you with open hearts. O Amma, please remove our pain.

Bhumi Devi ohne Dich
gibt es kein Leben
Bhumi Devi mit Dir
Wollen wir Leben

Bhumi Devi, without You there is no life. Bhumi Devi, we want to live with you.

gōvarddhanam uyartti (Malayalam)

gōvarddhanam uyartti kaṇṇan
indrande garvam aṭakki
gōpījana-prīyanāyi kaṇṇan
gōparipālakanāyi...

Kannan lifted the Govardhana mountain and subdued Indra's pride. Kannan was the beloved of the Gopis, and the protector of the cows.

kāḷiya-mardanam ceytu kaṇṇan
kāḷindiyil nṛttamāḍi
gōpikaḷ bhakti tannil kaṇṇan
rāsalīlayumāḍi

Kannan conquered the serpent, Kaliya, and danced the rasalila near the Kalindi river. Kannan danced with the gopis in their devotion.

vēṇuvil nādam mīṭṭi kaṇṇan
vēṇuvilōlanāyi
rādhatan tōzhanāyi kaṇṇan
rādhāramaṇanāyi

Enchanting all, Kannan became Venuvilola as he played His flute. As Radha's friend he became Radharamana (enchanter of Radha).

kamsavadham naḍatti kaṇṇan
ārtta-samrakṣakanāyi
dēvaki vasudēvare kaṇṇan
nityānandarākki

Kannan killed Kamsa and became the protector of the afflicted. Kannan made Devaki and Vasudeva eternally blissful.

draupadi mānam kāttu kaṇṇan
bhaktajanaprīyanāyi
pārtthande sārathiyāyi kaṇṇan
dharmatte tāṅgi nirtti

Kannan protected Draupadi's dignity, and became the beloved of the devotees. As Arjuna's charioteer, Kannan upheld dharma.

vēdārtthasāramāya gīta pālum
nukarnnu nalki
pāritu sarvattilum kaṇṇan
dharmabodham uṇartti

Krishna gave the milk that is the Gita, the essence of all the Vedas. Across the whole world, Kannan raised awareness about dharma.

kaṇṇā kaṇṇā kaṇṇā kaṇṇā kaṇṇā uṇṇi kaṇṇā
kaṇṇā kaṇṇā kaṇṇā kaṇṇā kaṇṇā ambāḍi kaṇṇā

Hakuna matata (Swahili)

hakuna matata na mama devi
anatupenda sote bila
kujali sifa mbaya tunazo
hasira wivu uchoyo tamaa

We have no worries with Mother Devi. She loves us all, no matter what negativities we have: anger, jealousy, greed or lust.

hakuna matata na mama devi
anajua mateso yetu na

anajaribu kutuongoza
huzuni ugonjwa aibu upweke

We have no worries with Mother Devi. She knows our suffering, our sorrow, disease, shame, loneliness – and tries to guide us.

hakuna matata na mama devi
fungua moyo wako na
umkaribishe kama mtoto
karibu sana, mama amma, moyoni, mwangu

We have no worries with Mother Devi. Open your heart and welcome Her like a child. Welcome Mother into your hearts!

mama amma, mama devi
mama amma, mama devi

Hana mo tori mo (Japanese)

hana mo, tori mo, kaze mo, umi mo
anata- o omotte, utai-masu
amma no ya sashii
ho hoemi omoi-naga-ra

Thinking of Mother's gentle smile, the flowers, the birds, the wind and the ocean all sing for you, .

dakara wata shi-mo aino-u-ta
issho-ni natte utaiimasu
amma no ya sashii
ho-hoemi omoi-naga-ra

I also want to sing a love-song, thinking of Mother's gentle smile.

sora mo tsuki mo hoshi mo- yama-mo
anata-o omotte utaa-imasu
amma no ya sashii
ho hoemi omoi-naga-ra

The sky, moon, stars and mountains also sing for you, thinking of Mother's gentle smile.

amma arigato, hontoni arigato
amma amma amma amma

Mother, thank you, thank you!

hara hara śiva śiva (Malayalam)

hara hara śiva śiva śaṅkara śambhō
caraṇam śaraṇam śrī śivaśambhō
hara hara śiva śiva śaṅkara śambhō
caraṇam śaraṇam śrī śivaśambhō

O Lord Shiva, victory to You! We take refuge at Your feet!

malamakaḷ puṇarum sundara gātram
malarsāyakane konnoru nētram
karatalam-atiloru bhikṣā-pātram
manamē! karutuka śivanē nityam

The daughter of the mountains (Parvati) embraces his beautiful body. His eyes burnt Kama (the God of Love) to ashes, and in His hand is a begging bowl. O mind, remain absorbed in Shiva always!

maññaṇi-malayuṭe mukaḷil nivāsam
mañjuḷa gaḷatala garaḷa-vilāsam

kāñjara varasutan antēvāsam
manamē! karutuka śambhu-vilāsam

His abode is the top of the snowy mountain. His lovely throat is blue from drinking deadly poison to save the world. He dwells in the hearts of Parasurama and Subramania. O mind! remain absorbed in Shiva.

phaṇigaṇa maṇḍana maṇḍita-rūpam
niṭila vilōcana nirgaḷa-tāpam
munijana vandita sundara-pādam
manamē! karutuka śivamaya rūpam

Snakes coil as ornaments around His body, and light emanates from the eye on His forehead. Sages adore His beautiful feet. O mind, remain absorbed in the form of Shiva!

vṛṣabha varō parihā sañcāram
tiruvuṭal niraye pūśān cāram
uraga gaṇam tiru-mārinu-hāram
manamē! karutuka śivam-ōmkāram

He travels on Vrishabha, the great bull. Sacred ash is smeared all over His body. A band of snakes coil around his neck as ornaments. O mind, become absorbed in the Omkara of Shiva!

cuṭalayil-iḷakum naṭana-viśēṣam
puliyuṭe tukalāl vastra-viśēṣam
uṭalil pakutiyum umayuṭe vēṣam
manamē! karutuka śaṅkara-vēṣam

He dances in the cremation grounds, and is clothed in a tiger skin. Half His body is the form of Uma [the Ardhanariswara form]. O mind, remain absorbed in the attire of Shiva!

hōli āyī dēkhō (Hindi)

hōli āyī dēkhō hōli āyī
vṛndāvan mēṅ āj hōli āyī
raṅg barsāne sab kā dil behlānē - vraja
vāsiyōṅ kē bīc āyā giridhāri

Holi has come! Look, Holi has come to Vṛndāvan! Lord Kṛṣṇa has come among the Vraj residents to shower holi colors on them and to make them all happy.

rādhā gōpiyōṅ gvālōṅ kē saṅg
hōli khēlē āj kṛṣṇa mōhan
śāmil hūē raṅg ḍhōl aur mṛdaṅg
jhūmē nācē gāyē vraj kā kaṇ kaṇ

Lord Kṛṣṇa has come to play Hōli with Rādha and the gōpis (milkmaids) and gōpas (cowherd boys). The celebrations pulsate with the drum beats of the dhol and mṛdang. Every atom in Vraj is dancing in bliss.

dēkhō hōli āyī! ō hōli āyī!

Look, Holi has come! O, Holi has arrived!

kānhā nē kī raṅgōṅ ki baucār
raṅg gayā sabkō raṅgōṅ sē āj
kisi kō bhī na chōḍē gōpāl
raṅg diyā usnē sabkō bār bār

Kṛṣṇa has sprayed colors and now everyone is streaked with Holi colors. He spared no one. Everyone is soaked with Hōli powder!

hōli kā aisā hūā āgman
bhakti kī uṭhī anōkhī taraṅg

kānhā nē aisā jādu kiyā
har liyā usnē lōgōṅ kā man

This spectacular Hōli celebration awakened devotion in the residents of Vraj. The Lord's exceptional splendor captivated all hearts.

jay jay giridhāri! jay jay śyām murāri!
hōli āyī, hōli āyī, dēkhō hōli āyī!

Hør Gud, hvor (Danish)

Hør Gud, hvor - jeglænges
Efter at mærke Dig imig
Mithjerte - det banker
Ogkalderhøjtpå Dig

O God, listen to my longing to feel You in my heart. My heart beats and calls out to You.

Blot endråbe
Var hvadjegfiksmagtaf Dig
Og nu kanjegikkefånok, nej
Mithjertetørsterefter Dig

Just one drop was all I tasted of You. And now I can't get enough. My heart is thirsting for You.

Somstjerner – inatten
Blinker ditøjetilmig
Du kalder - komtilmig
Lad migbliveét med dig

Like the stars in the night, Your eyes twinkle at me. You are calling. Come to me, let me merge in You!

Du ogjegerét
Lad mig se det -Du ogjegerét
Lad mig se det,
åh lad mig se det

You and I are one. Please let me see it, O please let me see it!

hṛdayattin aṭittaṭṭil (Malayalam)

hṛdayattin aṭittaṭṭil ninnoru rōdanam
entinenn-aṙiyilla ammē
ārārum kāṇāte ārārum kēḷkkāte
kaṇṇunīr puzhayāyi tēṅgalāyi

O Mother, from the depths of my heart arose a cry. I do not know why. Unseen and unheard, my tears became a river of lament.

ammatan vātsalyam nukaruvānō?
āliṅganattil amaruvānō?
ā pādapadmattil keṭṭipuṇarnnu ñān
śaraṇāgatikkāy kēṇiṭunnu

Was it to bask in Amma's affection? Or to be lost in her embrace? I cried for surrender, tightly hugging those lotus feet.

ninnuṭe sānniddhyam innende mānasam
śuddhi ceytīṭuvān kaniyukillē?
ammatan ōmanayāy māṙukillē? ammē
śuddhamām hṛdayattil nī varillē?

Mother, will you not be compassionate and purify my mind by your presence? Will I not become your darling child? O Mother, will you not come to the heart that has become pure?

Illumina el mey camí (Catalan)

Illumina el meu camí
Mare vina cap a mi
por tadora d'alegria
Tu ets el meu destí

Light up my way, Mother. Come to me as a bearer of joy. You are my destiny.

Oh mare divina!
Oh mare divina!
Oh mare divina!
Sempre estas al meu costat

O Divine Mother, You are always by my side.

Ens ensenyes la unitat
i la única veritat
la paciencia infinita
i la felicitat

You teach us unity, the only Truth, infinite patience, and happiness.

El teu rostre dola i bell
blau marí, fosc com el cel
Ocèa de compassió
creadora dels tres mons

Your sweet and beautiful face is deep blue, dark as the sky. Ocean of compassion, creator of the three worlds!

Ilumina ilumina (Spanish)

Ilumina ilumina señora querida
Ilumina mi mente con luz divina

O beloved Goddess, enlighten my mind with divine light!

Ilumina a tus hijos
Ilumina todo la creación
Océano de compasión,
ilumina o amma mi corazón

Shed light on your children, and on all of creation. Ocean of compassion, Mother, please enlighten my heart!

Señora eres el punto de luz
Dejame bañame en tus ojos
Guíame hasta mi destino
O amma tú eres mi camino

O Goddess, You are the point of light. Let me bathe in your eyes. Guide me to my destination, O Mother. You are my path!

Cantando el sagrado om
me fundo en tu forma infinita
Om... om... om...
O amma dejame ser tu estrellita

I chant the sacred syllable Om, and melt into your infinite form. Om, Om... O Mother, let me be your little star.

Ilumina amma ilumina me
Ilumina amma ilumina me

Enlighten me, O Mother! O Mother, enlighten me!

indranīladyutim (Sanskrit)

indranīladyutim śyāmavarṇṇam – lōlam
indīvarēkṣaṇam sundarākṣam
indusamam mugdha-cārugātram – dēvam
indrādi-vanditam pādayugmam

Lord Krishna, whose lustrous dark complexion is like blue sapphire, whose eyes are as charming as the blue lotus. His glance is gentle, and His face is beautiful as the full moon. Gods like Indra worship His divine feet.

mālēyacandana-carccitāṅgam – divya
mālyādalaṅkṛta vakṣōruham
makaranda-madhurita-mandahāsam – bhakta
mānasē bhāvanā-lōla rūpam

Sandal paste anoints the Lord's limbs, and fragrant garlands adorn His chest. His smile is as sweet as honey, and His form transports devotees into a meditative state.

gōrōcanāṅkita phālataṭam – dhanya
gōpikānanda-vilāsakandam
gōvatsa-pālana-sēvanārttham – puṇya
gōvarddhanōddhāram līlāmayam

Krishna's forehead is adorned with the mark of gōrōcana (a fragrant medicinal extract). He is the cause of the gopis' (milkmaids') happiness. The Lord enacted the divine sport of raising the Gōvardhana mountain to protect the cowherds.

bhāvanōllāsa-vilāsa-raṅgam – bhakta
hṛdaya-mandāralatā-nikuñjam
bhavarōga-tāraṇa vēṇunādam – bhakti
mukti-pradāyakam mantra-nādam

The hearts of devotees, tender as Mandara (the heavenly flower), are saturated in bliss from remembering the Lord. The sound of His flute helps overcome the miseries of the world, and its entrancing music bestows devotion and liberation.

In every heart (English)

In every heart, let us see
the flame of love, pure divinity.
We're children of one God,
embodiments of pure love.

Every nation, all creation,
happiness reaches everyone
all around the world. Joy embraces all.

Beyond all doubt, let us see
we are the same, one humanity.
Together let us rise,
breaking from our fear, our ties.

Io sono una bolla (Italian)

Io sono una bolla agitata dalle onde
Per andare sotto l'acqua Madre Mia come fare?

I am a bubble stirred by the waves. How to sink under water, O Mother?

Ho solo un desiderio con Te diventare Uno
Ascolta il mio cuore, io Ti chiamo con amore

To merge with You is my only desire. Listen to my heart. I am calling you with love

Amma, Amma, Amma vieni
Krishna, krishna, krishna vieni
Madre Mia come fare diventare uno con Te?
Galleggiare sotto l'acqua, nel blu profondo di Krishna

O Mother, how to merge with you? To float on water, in the deep blue of Krishna.

I see in this dark night (English)

I see in this dark night,
by your radiant light of love.
Please touch my lonely heart,
compassionate dear mother.

You are both god and goddess.
You are one, and you are all!

You are Saraswati, who teaches music.
You are Durga, who shows us the truth.
You are Lakshmi, showering love.
You are Parvati, mother to all.

You are both god and goddess.
You are one, and you are all!

You are Kali, who gives us courage.
You are Ganga, who makes us pure.
You are Shakti, giving us strength.
You are Amma, guru to all.
You are both god and goddess.

jab se pāvan (Hindi)

jab se pāvan man mandir mēṅ
prīt rām kī pālī hai
rāt sunehari din mēṅ hōlī
rāt divālī hai, rāt divālī hai

Since the day I nurtured the love for lord Rama in the temple of my heart, my mornings have become golden. My days are like Holi (Indian festival of colors), my nights are like Diwali (Indian festival of lights).

antarvāsī kō khōju kyūṅ
idhar udhar bāhar mēṅ
viṣay vikārōṅ kē bandhan hī
lāyē is duniyā mē
gyān kī daulat kō pā mēnē
har ik daulat pālī hai
har ik daulat pālī hai
rāt dīvālī hai, rāt divālī hai

Why search outside for the one who dwells within. Our attachment to objects and our desires bind us to this world. By receiving the wealth of knowledge I have received all wealth.

rām bhaj man rām bhaj man rām rām rām
rām bhaj man rām bhaj man rām rām rām
jay śrī rām jay śrī rām jay śrī rām jay śrī rām

janam maraṇ dharmōṅ karmōṅ kē
rām vidhān banāyē
kēval ātmagyān kē khātir
palpal jag srijāyē
ant nahīṅ unkī karuṇā kā
yah sṛṣṭī nirālī hai
yah sṛṣṭī nirālī hai
rāt divālī hai, rāt divālī hai

Rama sets the principles of birth, death, dharma and karma. Rama creates the world only for the attainment of Self-knowledge. Infinite indeed is His Compassion, unique indeed His Creation.

jagadīśvarī mā (Malayalam)

jagadīśvarī mā jagadīśvarī mā
jagadīśvarī mā jagadīśvarī mā

O Mother goddess, Mother of the world!

ammē en uḷḷil teḷiyēṇamē
ammē nin kṛpa coriyēṇamē

O Mother, please shine within, and shower Your grace!

ammē nin upakaraṇam ākkēṇamē
ammē nin kaṭākṣam coriyēṇamē

O Mother, please make me Your instrument, and grace me with Your sidelong glance.

ammē nin iccha en iccha ākaṇe
ammē nin pādattil aliyēṇamē

Please, may Your will be my will, and merge me in Your divine feet!

jaya rama rama ram (French)

jaya rama rama ram jaya rama rama ram
jaya rama rama ram jay jay ram

Victory to Lord Rama!

protecteur du dharma
doux époux de Sita
tu me montres la voie

Protector of dharma, tender husband of Sita, You show me the way.

O toi Rama
si noble roi
tu me donnes la foi

O Rama, most noble king, you grant me faith.

ta prière est ma lumière
ta victoire est ma gloire
ton courage, mon sillage
ta voie, ma joie

Your prayer is my light, your victory my glory, your courage my waking, your way my joy.

jay ram jay ram jay jay ram
jay ram jay ram jay jay ram

o rama... o rama... o rama... o rama...

jay jay dēvi (Sanskrit)

jay jay dēvi jay jay durgē jay jay kāḷi mā

ammē dēvi ānanda-dāyini ādiparāśakti mā
akhilāṇḍēśvarī abhaya-pradāyini ātma-svarūpiṇi mā

dēvi mātā jagatkāriṇi jagadīśvari jay jay
dēvi mātā jagatpālini jaganmayi jay jay

durgē mātā śivaśaṅkari śaktidāyini mā
durgē mātā śubhakāriṇi śāntidāyini mā

kāḷi bhavatāriṇi bhayahāriṇi jay jay
kāḷi bhaktarakṣaki bhuvanēśvari jay jay

jay rām sītāpatē (Sanskrit)

jay rām śrī rām sītāpatē rām

daśaratha nandana rām
kausalya suta rām
lakṣmaṇa sōdara rām
ayodhya vāsī rām

jay śrīrām sītāpatē rām
hanumat sēvita rām

sarvajanapriya rām
rāvaṇāntaka rām
trilōka pālaka rām

śrī rām jay rām
śrī rām jay rām
śrī rām jay rām jay rām

Je suis un rayon (French)

Je suis un rayon, Tu es le Soleil
Je suis une étoile, Tu es la Lumière
Je suis un nuage, Tu es le Ciel
Je suis une vague, Tu es l'Océan
Je suis une fleur, Tu es la Terre
Je suis un cœur, Tu es l'Amour

I am a ray, You are the sun. I am a star, You are its light. I am a cloud, You are the sky. I am a wave, You are the ocean. I am a flower, You are the Earth. I am a heart, You are love.

Je suis ici, Tu es partout
Je suis Toi, Tu es Moi
Je suis Toi, Tu es Moi
nous sommes un, nous sommes un

I am here, You are everywhere. I am You, You are me, we are one.

Je suis un sourire, Tu es la Joie
Je suis le calme, Tu es la Paix
Je suis l'étincelle, Tu es la Flamme

Je suis vivant, Tu es la Vie
Je suis un atome, Tu es l'Univers
Je suis en Toi, Tu es en Moi

I am a smile, You are joy. I am calm, You are peace. I am a spark, you are the flame. I am alive, You are life. I am an atom, You are the Universe. I am in You, You are in me.

Je suis un enfant, Tu es ma Mère

I am a child, You are my Mother.

jag spandan (Hindi)

jag spandan sat kā bas ēk sat hai
śabda aur vṛtti sē āvṛt cit hai
maun acal sthir satvastu hai tū
tanmē manaḥ śiv-sankalpam-astu

This creation is nothing but vibration of Sat (Truth). Chit (consciousness) becomes as if covered by word and thought. You are ever silent, immanent and changeless! May such benevolent and beautiful thoughts fill my mind!

brahma-jyōti man kuch nahīṅ apnā
jāgrat aur svapn sabhī sapnā
satatam samāhi turīya tatva tū
tanmē manaḥ śiv-sankalpam-astu

It's the light of Brahma, not that of the mind. Waking, dreaming and deep sleep are all dreams only. The tureeya (fourth) alone is the constant substratum of all three states. May such benevolent and beautiful thoughts fill my mind!

ēk jyōti sarvatra samāyī
śivā yahāṅ sab nahīṅ jīv kōyī
advait jagā dvait chōḍ tū
tanmē manaḥ śiv-sankalpam-astu

A single light of lights shines everywhere. Everything and being is not a separate entity but Shiva alone. Removing the sense of duality, let us wake up in non-duality! May such benevolent and beautiful thoughts fill my mind!

kartā nahīṅ ham kāraṇ mātr sab
ēk hī tatva kē amś ham sab
miṭā kartāpan tadrūp hō tū
tanmē manaḥ śiv-sankalpam-astu

We are not the doer; we are only instruments in His hands. All of us are parts of that One whole. Abandoning the sense of doership, let us identify with that Shiva principle. May such benevolent and beautiful thoughts fill my mind!

Jai jai mukunda (Spanish)

jai jai mukunda, jai jai mukunda
o krishna! jai krishna!
keshava, madhava
govinda, gopala
jai jai mukunda, jai jai mukunda
Tú, que júgabas con las gopís
robando su mantequilla

You, who played with the Gopis, and stole their butter.

Ven aquí yo te he de acariciar
Yo tengo mantequilla para ti robár

Come here that I may caress You. I have butter for You to steal.

Yo te espero con una guirnalda
de flores frescas. ¿No vienes?

I await You with a garland of fresh flowers. Won't You come?

Krishná, fuénte de amor,
sálvame, réscatame del océano de deseós

O Krishna, source of love, save me! Rescue me from the ocean of desires.

kali devi jaganmata (Sanskrit)

kali devi jaganmata
kali devi jaganmata
jago devi jaganmata
jago devi jaganmata

jay ho jay ho
jaganmata

devi mata durge mata
jago devi jaganmata
amma jago jay jay mata
amma jago jay jay mata

kāḷi devi amme parāśakti
kālātīte kāḷimāte

jagannāthe jagadambe
premarūpe parātpare
jñānarūpe dayānidhe

śivaśakti svarūpini
kāle bhakti pradāyini
sarvaduḥkha vināśini
sarvaloka nirañjini

kāḷi kāḷi kapālini (Sanskrit)

kāḷi kāḷi kapālini
kālabhaya-nivāriṇi
triguṇa-rūpiṇi annadāyini
trinētra-dhāriṇi ādikāriṇi

O Kali, You destroy the fear of death. You are the form of the three gunas, and You are the giver of nourishment. You have three eyes and are the primal cause.

jay jay kāḷi mahākāḷi
kāḷi kāḷi jay jay

purahara manamōhini
muṇḍamāla suśōbhini
tattva-dāyini śyāma-sundari
trāṇa-kāriṇi amara-pālini

Destroyer of the three puras, You are the enchanter of my mind. You are divinely resplendent with Your garland of skulls. You grant knowledge and are beautiful with Your dark complexion. You are the protector and the eternal one.

kālarātri svarūpiṇi
duḥkha-dāridra nāśini
raktabīja vināśini
ahaṅkāra vināśini

You are the form of night and the destroyer of unhappiness and poverty. You killed the demon Raktabija, and are the destroyer of the ego.

kāḷī karāḷī mahāśakti (Sanskrit)

kāḷī karāḷī mahāśakti śaṅkarī
śrībhadrakāḷī jaya jaya (jaya jaya)
aimkārī hrīmkārī kḷīmkārī śrīmkāri
śrībhuvanēśvarī jaya jaya (jaya jaya)

jaya jaya kāḷī
prēmabhaktim mē dēhī
jaya jaya kāḷī
mām pātu cāmuṇḍī

śumbhaniśumbhāsura ghātinīdēvī
śrīśailavāsinī jaya jaya
madhumarddinī mahiṣāsuramarddinī
śrī tripurasundarī jaya jaya (jaya jaya)

bhayahāriṇī bhavatāriṇī bhairavī
śrīmahākāḷī jaya jaya
ādi anādī ananta mahēśvarī
śrī paramēśvarī jaya jaya (jaya jaya)

Kali mata zai (Chinese)

kali mata zai hu huan

Kali mata is calling.

Rénshēng cōngcōng yòu duǎnzàn
rénmen què zhuī zhú jìnghuā shuǐyuè
Zhǐ luòde jīn pí lì jié yīshēn fánnǎo bùnéng jiě

Life is busy and short, but people chase illusions like the moon in the water. In the end, only exhaustion and unsolvable suffering remain.

Bì yǎn qīngtīng yīqiè zài nǐ xīnzhōng
Nǐ zhuīxún de yīqiè yuányú zì xìng
Shèngmǔ qǐng ni zhǐchū nà yǒnghéng de zhēnlǐ

Close your eyes and listen. Everything is inside you. All that you seek comes from the effulgent Self. Divine Mother, please point out that eternal Truth!

kāṇān-uzharunna (Malayalam)

kāṇān-uzharunna kaṇṇumāy-amma-tan
kāliṇa kūppunnu makkaḷ – kaṇṇu-
nīrumāyi kākkunnu makkaḷ
kāruṇya-pūram coriyuma kaṇṇiṇa
kāṇān kotikkunnu makkaḷ – pāda-
pūjaykk-uzharunnu makkaḷ

O Mother! Your children long to see You. Their eyes constantly seek Your presence. With tears in their eyes, Your children salute Your lotus feet! They long to see Your dark eyes that send forth streams of compassion. They long to worship Your lotus feet!

mātrakaḷkk-entoru nīḷamāṇ-ammaye
mātram smariccirikkumbōḷ
kāṇāt-akannirikkumbōḷ
māsaṅgaḷ mātrakaḷ-āyirunn-ammaye
mātramāy kaṇḍirunnappōl – amma
cāratt-aṇaññ-irunnappōḷ

Lost in memories of You, separated from You, each moment seems like forever. The months flew by like moments when You were beside us, when our eyes drank in Your divine presence.

bāhyayām-ammayall-ammayenn-amma-tan
snēhārdramām mozhi satyam – prēma-
mūrttiyām-ammatan satyam
bāhyayallamma tann-ātmāvu tān-enna
sādhanaykk-amma tan mārgam – śōka
mōham-akattunna mārgam

"The real Amma is not this external form." Your loving words ring true for us, O Mother, the embodiment of love. Through this, You illumine the path of sadhana that removes all delusion and unhappiness. We realize our true Self by finding the inner Amma.

eṅkilum-ammē! dayāmayi vēgam-onn-
iṅgu vannālum-īvēnal – ammē
nin nizhal-illātta vēnal
eṅgane makkaḷ sahikkum, sudhā-varṣam
onn-iṅgu peyt-aṇaññālum! ammē
eṅgum kuḷirma peytālum

Even so, Compassionate Mother, please come to us soon! Pour down as ambrosial rain to cool the unbearable heat of this summer, bereft of the shade of your presence. O Mother, pour down as cool, reviving rains!

Kang a yo i wei (Chinese)

Kang a yo i wei shen shung mo-o tchin
Chu iu jen ay wang jee tzu jee
Devi lie dao woa min je jong
Yung bao jen-lay lee-ow iu shang tong

Look, there is the Divine Mother. Out of love She forgot herself. Devi came among us to embrace humanity and heal its wounds.

Shen eye, tchi dao, fo-o, chang song, see-ow

Love, pray, serve, chant and smile. Love deeply. Pray, serve, chant (the Scriptures), smile.

Devi lie-ling huang sing jong jen
choo chou waje fong fay sing ling
Sw-eh hwey ming see-ang eye hu tze-jon
Zt-eye devi sing lee wamen shu ee-tee

Devi came to awaken us, to remove our ego, and free our minds/souls. Learn to meditate. Protect nature. We are one in Devi's heart!

kanivoṭakaṭṭuka (Malayalam)

kanivoṭ-akaṭṭuka pratibandham
kaṇi kāṇmatināy nin rūpam
azhakind-atbhuta malarallē nī
agatikk-ālambanam allē

O compassionate one, remove all the obstacles that prevent me from seeing your form. You are the wondrous flower of beauty, the refuge for helpless souls.

manninu kiṭṭiya nidhiyallē... nī
puṇyam kāyccoru kaniyallē
kaṇṇinu kāntikkatirallē... en
karaḷinu nī tūvamṛtallē

You are the treasure received by the earth. You are the fruit of meritorious deeds. You are the beautiful ray of light to my eyes. You are ambrosia for my heart.

bhārata-bhāgya vidhātākkaḷ
tēṭi orudgīthapporuḷē
vēdiccāl-aṙiyum nīyulakinu
kālam nalkiya kāṇiykka

You are the essence of the Vedas, sought by the great sages of Bharata. The knowledgeable ones know that you are the gift that Time has given to the world.

bhuvanam tazhukum kāruṇyam
atulitam-ākum mahattyāgam
jñānam bhaktiyat-ellām-ottoru
vaibhavam-āṇī mātṛtvam

Compassion that caresses the world, sacrifice beyond compare, the unity of supreme knowledge and devotion. This glorious motherhood is the fullness of all these.

janmam koṇḍoru kathayuṇḍō
cinmayi nin padam aṇayāykil?
janmāntara-sukṛtattālallē
brahmānandam-iyannīṭū!

O Chinmayi! Of what use is this life if I do not reach your feet? One can experience supreme bliss only through the merit gained from the good deeds of many previous lives

cāratt-eppozhum uṇḍēlum
cētassil teḷivillāykil
kāṇill-ammaye nēril orālpparam
ānandāmṛta-bhāvattil

Even though Mother is close, it is impossible for us to see Her in the form of Infinite Bliss if our mind is not pure.

kāṇmatil-ellām nin rūpam
kāṇān kaṇṇu kotikkunnu
uḷḷam viṅgi piṭayunn-ennuṭe
uḷḷattil kaṇi kaṇḍīṭān

My eyes long to see you everywhere. My heart aches to see you within me.

kaṇṇane kāṇān (Malayalam)

kaṇṇane kāṇān uzhalunnu en manam
kaṇṇanāyi kaṇṇīr-ozhukiṭunnu

My mind pines to see Kannan [Krishna]. My tears are flowing profusely for Kannan.

oru nōkku kāṇuvān oru vākku kēḷkkuvān
kaṇṇa nī arikil varikayillē?
etra yugaṅgaḷāy kāttirikkunnu ñān
tṛppāda-darśanam nalkukillē?

That I may catch a glimpse of you, that I may hear a word from you, O Kanna, will you not come close to me? How many eons have I waited for the vision of your divine feet?

kāruṇya-vāridhē kārmukil varṇṇā nī
en hṛdayattil vasikkukillē?
kamala nētrā! nin mukham kāṇuvān
enikk-oralpam bhāgyam nalkukillē?

Ocean of compassion, O Kanna, of the color of rain-clouds, will You not dwell in my heart? O lotus-eyed one! Won't you grant me a little good fortune, that I may see your face?

citta cōrā ende uṇṇikaṇṇā
ponkāl cilambu ñān keṭṭi tarām
nṛttamāṭān nī varukayillē? ennōṭ-
oppamāṭān nī varukayillē?

Stealer of my heart, my little Kanna! I will adorn your darling feet with gold anklets. Will you not come to dance with me?

kaṇṇā nī ōṭi vāyō (Malayalam)

kaṇṇā nī ōṭi vāyō ōṭakkuzhal ūti vāyō
ennuḷḷil kuṭikoḷḷu kaṇṇā kaṇṇā
uṇṇikkaṇṇā kaṇṇā (2)

O Kanna, come running, playing your flute! Come and dwell within me, dear little Kanna!

kārvarṇṇan gōkulapālan
sakhimārum gōkkaḷumāyi
ambōṭṭi maṭiyil vāyō
kaṇṇā kaṇṇā uṇṇikkaṇṇā kaṇṇā

O Kanna, of the color of rainclouds, protector of Gokula! With your little friends and the cows, come running to mother's lap, my dear little Kanna!

kaṇṇan vannīṭukil pāl veṇṇa cōru tarām
maṇṇappam cuṭṭu kaḷikkām
kaṇṇā kaṇṇā uṇṇikkaṇṇā kaṇṇā

O Kanna, if you come, I will give you milk, butter and rice. We can play together making mud-cakes, my dear little Kanna!

kaṇṇunnīru tumbi (Badaga)

kaṇṇunnīru tumbi sūsirā
idā toḍavuduga en amma illayā

When my tears are overflowing, isn't Mother here to wipe them?

nā ena pāpamāḍidēntu
nī enna nōḍādē ī budugā
nā ī lōkanā... paḍōpāḍu nōḍi ninaga gava bappillayā
ammā... ammā... ninaga gava illayā... gava illayā

What mistake did I commit for You not to look at me? Seeing me caught in this world, do You not feel compassion, O Mother?

innu ēsagā janma – nā
uṭṭodu ninanā noḍuduga
nīnāga sēvā... māḍīntu idanē nā ini uṭṭade ibudugā
ammā... ammā... uṭṭāde ibuduga... etē ammā

How many births must I take to be able to see You? I will perform Your seva, to avoid being born again, O Mother.

badiksī buḍūnī badiksī buḍūnī
enna kai buḍātē
ammā... ammā... kai buḍātē

Come Mother, bless me, please bless me. Do not leave me!

karayāt-endōmana (Malayalam)

karayāt-endōmana paitalē
kaṇṇīr tuṭaykkām endārōmalē
ammaykku nī ennum kaṇṇāṇu karaḷāṇu
ammatan pūmaṭi ennum ninakkāṇu
rārō rārō rārārō

Do not cry, my darling child. I will wipe away your tears. You are mother's heart and her eyes. Mother's lap is always there for you.

ārīram pāṭīṭām ammayennum
ārōmalē nī uṙaṅguṙaṅgu

Amma will always sing you a lullaby, my sweet child. Go to sleep.

kuṭṭikkuṙumbukaḷ kāṭṭi nī ettumbōḷ
cāññum cariññum nī ammaye nōkkumbōḷ
nī aṙiyāte nin ninavaṙiyāte

kaivaḷarunnō mey taḷarunnō
ennamma nōkki nilpu ōmalē
amma kāttu nilppū

As you come near me in all your mischief, as you twirl and turn and peep at mother, secretly, she looks to see if you are growing strong and tall. My darling, mother waits for that day.

paraduḥkham kāṇavē kaṇṇīr pozhiccitān
ñān enna bhāvam-illāymayil nīntiṭān
kāruṇyāmṛta-dhārayāy peytiṭān
nirmala prēmavum nistula-tyāgavum
nīyāy māṙīṭaṇam amma tan
antaḥraṅgam kotippū

Mother's heart longs for Her child to grow as one who will shed tears at the sorrow of others, who will swim along in life without being pulled down by ego, who will rain down as showers of compassion, who will become pure love and perfect renunciation.

karimukil varṇṇā (Malayalam)

karimukil varṇṇā kaṭal varṇṇā
kālccilambin kiṅgiṇi nādam
kanakamaṇimaya nūpura-mēḷam
kāttiṭunnen hṛdayakavāṭam

O Krisha, the color of dark rain clouds, of the deep blue ocean, the doors of my heart are protected by the tinkling of your golden anklets.

kaṇḍukaṇḍen uḷḷam takadhimi
kēṭṭukēṭṭen kātukaḷ taka taka

koṭṭiṭaṭṭe kaikaḷ kiṭataka
kāttiṭunnen hṛdayakavāṭam

Seeing your dancing anklets, my heart goes 'takadhimi'. My ears go 'takataka'. Let your hands beat 'kidataka', as they protect the doors of my heart.

kaikaḷil tarivaḷakaḷum-iṭṭu
kātilōla kammalum-iṭṭu
kālkaḷil cilambukaḷiṭṭu
kāttiṭunnen hṛdayakavāṭam

You wear bangles on your wrists and dangling ear rings. You wear the heavy chilambu anklets on your feet, as you protect the doors of my heart.

añjanakkal añjanamāy
kari-mizhikaḷilāy ezhuti
kāṙoḷikk-okkum tirumēni
kāttiṭunnen hṛdayakavāṭam

Guard the doors of my heart with your lovely dark eyes lined with anjanam (collyrium), and your body that resembles a dark cloud.

kāṙoḷi varṇṇā... harē kṛṣṇā
kārmukil varṇṇā... śrīkṛṣṇā
vāsudēvā... harē kṛṣṇā
dēvakinandana... śrīkṛṣṇā
śyāmavarṇṇā... harē kṛṣṇā
mēghavarṇṇā... śrīkṛṣṇā
nandakumārā... harē kṛṣṇā
navanītacōrā... śrī kṛṣṇā
jayahari kṛṣṇā... jay kṛṣṇā

jay śrīkṛṣṇā... śrīkṛṣṇā
harē harē kṛṣṇā... harē kṛṣṇā
harē śrīkṛṣṇā... śrīkṛṣṇā
harē harē kṛṣṇā... harē kṛṣṇā
harē śrīkṛṣṇā... śrīkṛṣṇā

kṛṣṇa kṛṣṇa hari gōvindā
kṛṣṇa kṛṣṇa hari gōpālā

karuṇārdra mānasē (Malayalam)

karuṇārdra mānasē kāruṇya mūrttē
en ambikē amṛtāmbikē
kōmaḷē kāḷi bhavatāriṇi ambē
bhaktapriyē amṛtāmbikē

O my mother, eternal mother, embodiment of mercy, whose heart melts with compassion! Tender one, Kali, who carries us across the ocean of samsara. Mother, dear to the devotees, eternal mother!

tṛyambakē tripurātmikē sarvalōkēśi
nin kazhal ñān vandikkunnēn
mānava ṛṣīśvar stutikkumā trikkazhal
ñānitā vandiciṭunnēn
bhuvanēśvari amṛtāmbikē

O Mother of the three cities, goddess of all the worlds, I bow down at your feet. I bow down before your sacred feet that are praised by the rishis. O goddess of the Earth, eternal goddess!

muktirūpi prēmarūpiṇi māyē ni
ennil kṛpacoriyēṇē

īśvararkkum īśvarī nin tiru rūpam
darśikkaṇam enikkammē
tripurēśvari amṛtāmbikē

You are mukti (liberation), embodiment of divine love, divine illusion. Please shower your grace upon me! Goddess of the gods, please grant me the vision of Your sacred form. O goddess of the three cities, eternal goddess!

śāradē śaṅkari śrīkari śāmbhavi
ennuḷḷil nī vasikkēṇē
ennaham-bōdham keṭutti nī mānasē
śraddhayum bōdhavum nalku
jagadīśvari amṛtāmbikē

O Mother Saraswati, Shankari, Srikari, please dwell within me. Remove my sense of 'I', and bestow faith and awareness in my mind. O goddess of the world, eternal goddess!

kāruṇyarūpiṇi ammē nin (Malayalam)

kāruṇyarūpiṇi ammē nin
kṛpāmṛtam coriyū
nin pādapatmattil cēruvān
kṛpāmṛtam coriyū

O Mother, embodiment of compassion, please shower Your grace that I may merge in Your feet.

nin prēmadhārayil nīṇti-kkaḷikkunnu
ninnuḍe makkaḷammē
niṣkaḷa-prēmavum nirmala-bhaktiyum

ēki nī ninnil cērkkū – ammē
ēki nī ninnil cērkkū

Mother, Your children swim and play in the torrent of Your love. Granting innocent love and pure devotion, please draw us to You.

nin maṭittaṭṭil ennum kiṭakkuvān
enne anugrahikkū
nin sudhāmṛtam makkaḷil tūki
ānanda-magnarākkū – ammē
ānanda-magnarākkū

Bless me always to lie on Your lap. Shower Your ambrosia on Your children, immerse them in bliss, O Mother!

nin pādaspandanam kēḷkkān kotikkunnu
ninnuḍe kuññumakkaḷ
nin sundararūpam ennuḍe hṛttil
uṇḍākaṇē dēvī – ennennum
uṇḍākaṇe dēvī

Your little children long to hear the sound of Your footsteps. O Devi, may Your beautiful form ever shine in our hearts.

kāttaruḷvāy dēvi (Tamil)

kāttaruḷvāy dēviyē satgatipradāyini
un kuzhantayai kāttaruḷvāy

O Devi, you guide us towards the right path. Protect and bless your child!

nilayillā poruḷil nimmati tēṭi
pōkāmal ennai nī kāttaruḷvāy ammā

O Mother, protect me so that I don't chase after ephemeral things looking for peace.

etirppārppillāmal anpai anaivarukkum
taruvatarkku
aruḷpurivāy kāruṇya rūpiṇiyē

O Devi, personification of compassion, bless me to love everyone without any expectations!

seykindra karmam ellām pūjayāka
seytiṭa aruḷ purivāy dēviyē

O Devi, bless me to do all my actions with devotion.

anaittuyirkkum nimmatiyum nambikkaiyum
tantaruḷvāy sarvēśvarī ammā

O Mother, supreme goddess, grant peace and faith to all beings and bless us all!

bhakti tā jagadambē
anpai tā jagadambē
nambikkai tantennai
kāttiṭuvāy jagadambē

O Goddess of the universe, give me devotion, give me love, give me faith and protect me.

kātyāyani dēvi (Hindi)

kātyāyani dēvi mahāgauri, mahīṣamarddini pārvati mā
śailaputri tū gauri mā, tripura-sundari dēvi mā

O Mother Katyayani, Devi, destroyer of the demon Mahisha. Goddess Parvati! You are Gauri, the daughter of the mountain, and Devi, the beautiful goddess of the three cities.

mēri pyāri ambā mā, pyāri pyāri mēri ambā mā

My dear mother, my dear dear mother!

kālarātri ō kāḷi mā, ghanakēśi hē trinayani mā
mērē duḥkhōṅ kō har lē, pāpanāśini bhairavi mā

You are Kali, the dark night, O three-eyed Mother with dark hair! Please remove my sorrow, O Mother Bhairavi, destroyer of sin!

mēri pyāri kāḷi mā, pyāri pyāri mēri kāḷi mā

My dear mother Kali, my dear dear mother Kali!

candraghaṇṭ tū vaiṣṇavi mā, candra jaisē hi camkē mā
mērē man kō karō nirmal, sukh pradāyini sundari mā

O Goddess Chandraghanta (name of Durga), you are Mother Vaishnavi. You are radiant as the moon. Please purify my mind, O beautiful mother who bestows joy!

mēri pyāri vaiṣṇō mā, pyāri pyāri mēri vaiṣṇō mā

My dear mother Vaishnavi, my dear dear mother Vaishnavi

jay jay mā ambē mā, jay jay mā jagadambē mā

Victory to mother, victory to the mother of the world!

Kmo navad hatoe (Hebrew)

kmo navad hatoe bashmama
lifnei geshem rishon, haadama

Like a wanderer lost in the desert. Like soil before the first rain.

gam bi, bore neshama
gam bi ten tsama

In me too, O creator of my soul, place that thirst.

tsama lo irveh
shel lev mekave

A thirst that can't be quenched in a hopeful heart.

veshelo yimale veshelo itratse
ad shenoten hatsama beatsmo yimatse
ad shenoten hatsama beatsmo yimatse

And let it not be quenched, and let it not be appeased until the giver of the thirst himself is found.

Kokoroyo nanio (Japanese)

kokoro yo, nani o, osorete iru noka
yuuki o kokoro ni, genki de warai
shiawase eran de ikina sai

O mind, what are you afraid of? Be courageous and cheerful. Smile. Choose to be happy.

Hitori kiri...
Aenu omoi ni shizumu toki
Amma ga, daki shimete
Oshi-ete kureta

I was all alone, buried in the sadness of not seeing Her. Then Amma embraced me and imparted these teachings.

Kokoro no yowasa, kizuita toki niwa
Nintai zuyoku, ayamachi naoshi
Tadashii kotoba de, kaki naose

Understanding the weakness of my mind, patiently correct my fault, and replace it with the proper words.

Yuuyakega...
Nureru kono hoho, someru toki Amma ga, daki shimete
Oshi-ete kureta

The sunset colored my wet cheeks, then Amma embraced me and imparted these teachings.

Shizen no inochi, taisetsu ni omou
Sekai no heiwa o, Inori masu
Arayuru chigai o, nori koete

Respect all life in Nature. Overcome all differences, pray for world peace.

Itoshikute...
Namida tomaranu, yume no naka

Amma ga, daki shimete
Oshi-ete kureta
Amma ga, daki shimete
Oshi-ete kureta

Missing Her so much, I dreamed I cried uncontrollably. Then Amma embraced me and imparted these teachings.

Kom hjem mit barn (Danish)

Kom hjem mit barn, kom hjem til mig
Tårer falder, jeg er hos dig

Come home my child, come home to me. Tears are falling. I am with you!

Kom hjem mit barn, kom hjem til mig
Amma er lige her, mit dejlige barn
Amma er lige her, mit dejlige barn
Amma er lige her, vær ikke bange

Come home my child, come home to me. Amma is right here, my darling child. Amma is right here, don't be afraid.

Verdens natur, alt går i ring
Det der bliver skabt, går bort igen
Alt du ejer, er væk en dag
Giv slip på det, og kom tilbage

The nature of the world is that everything goes in circles. What is created is later destroyed. Everything you own goes one day. Let it go, and come back.

Verden du ser, er fantasi
Luk dine øjne, gå indeni
Hold fast i mig, vær kærlighed
Vil være hos dig, til evig tid

The world you see is fantasy. Close your eyes and go inside. Cling to me and be love. I'll be with you for eternity.

Kom tillsammans (Swedish)

Kom tillsammans,
låt oss mötas,
vi behöver bry oss om
I kärlek vi är
ett o samma jag

Get together, let us meet. We need to care for each other. In love we are one and the same.

Vem kan du vara, vad kan du ge
En vacker tanke, ett leende
Leva i kärlek med Amma

Who can you be and what can you give? A loving thought and a smiling face. Live in love with Amma. Live in love with God.

Kom tillsammans
Ensamheten
försvinner här med dej
I närvaro vi är
Ett med dej, Amma

Get together. Loneliness disappears here with you. Right now, we are one with You Amma.

Vi längtar
Efter känslan,
Stämningen hos Amma
Närmare varandra,
närmare dej, Amma

We long to feel the atmosphere near Amma. Closer to each other, closer to the mother, live in love with Amma.

koṇḍāṭṭamām (Tamil)

koṇḍāṭṭamām koṇḍāṭṭam engaḷ vīṭṭil koṇḍāṭṭam
kuṭṭi kaṇṇan vandānē manadai koḷḷai koṇḍānē

Let's celebrate! Let's celebrate! In our house, let's have a celebration. Little Krishna has come, stealing our minds.

piñcu pādam mella vaittu salangai kuluṅga vandānē
pītāmbaram paṭṭuṭutti mālai cūḍi vandānē

Step slowly with your soft feet. Come, let us hear the tinkling of your anklets. Come, wearing a yellow silk cloth and a flower garland!

kṛṣṇā mukunda murare jaya kṛṣṇā mukunda murare

veṇṇaiyum pālum vaittunakku murukkum sīḍayum seytēnē
āsayāga ūṭṭi viṭṭu manam magizhntu ninḍrēnē

I have kept butter, milk and your favorite snacks for you. With so much love, I will feed you and watch you eat them with delight.

oḍi āḍi viḷayāḍi maraintiruntu azha vaittu
kāṇāmal tuḍikka vaittāy kaṇṇā - unnai
kāṇāmal tuḍikka vaittāy kaṇṇā

Running and dancing around, we played hide and seek. You make me cry when you hide from me!

ninaivellām kṛṣṇā kṛṣṇā ennuḷḷē vasikkum kṛṣṇa kṛṣṇa
kurai ondrum enakkillai kṛṣṇā - oru
kurai ondrum enakkillai kṛṣṇā

My thoughts are filled with 'Krishna Krishna'. My heart is filled with 'Krishna Krishna'. I have no worries when you are here!

kṛṣṇā kṛṣṇā dēvakī nandana (Sanskrit)

kṛṣṇā kṛṣṇā dēvakī nandana rādhē kṛṣṇā
kṛṣṇā kṛṣṇā mādhava mōhana rādhē kṛṣṇā

gōkulabāla gōparipāla rādhē kṛṣṇā
sundararūpa nandakumāra rādhē kṛṣṇā

nārāyaṇa vāsudēva rādhē kṛṣṇā
janārdana jagannāyaka rādhē kṛṣṇā

jagadīśvara paripālaya rādhē kṛṣṇā
suravandita paripālaya rādhē kṛṣṇā
kṛṣṇā śyāmavarṇā cittacōrā pāhi kṛṣṇā

kāḷiyamardana kamsaniṣūdana rādhē kṛṣṇā
dēvādhidēva dānavanāśana rādhē kṛṣṇā

kṛṣṇā śyāmavarṇā cittacōrā pāhi kṛṣṇā

kṛṣṇā kṛṣṇā rādhē kṛṣṇā
kṛṣṇā kṛṣṇā gōpī kṛṣṇā
kṛṣṇā kṛṣṇā nīla kṛṣṇā
kṛṣṇā kṛṣṇā mōhana kṛṣṇā

krishna krishna jay jay (Chinese)

krishna krishna, jay jay krishna, gen wo yi qi wan

Krishna Krishna, Victory to Krishna. Krishna is playing with me

yi er san mu tou ren, shui ye bu xu dong
krishna shuo wo men yong yuan zai yi qi
qu da guan zi ba, hoy!

"One two three statue! Nobody moves" (traditional game in China). Krishna says we are together forever. Let's go break the pots (of butter)!

krishna zai, jiu bu pa, da jia wan qi lai
krishna shuo shen me, wo jiu ting shen me
wo xin ren ni krishna, wo xin ren ni jay

I'm not afraid because Krishna is here. Let's play together. Whatever Krishna says, I'll just follow his words. I trust you Krishna, I trust you. Jay!

krishna krishna jay jay krishna
krishan krishna jay jay jay

kṛṣṇā, nī ennil (Malayalam)

kṛṣṇā, nī ennil varum ennōrttu
tṛṣṇayōṭ-innum kāttirikkunnu ñān
nin muḷantaṇḍinde īṇamāyi ñān
nindēt-ākān koticciṭunnu

Krishna! I long for you to arrive in my heart. I yearn to be a melody in your flute and merge in you.

nī varilleṅkil niścalam en janmam
kaṇṇīr-kkaṭalilāy āzhnnu pōkum
mukiline pulkān pulkkoṭi kotikkil
varṣamāyi peytiṙaṅgīṭēṇḍē nī – kṛṣṇā

If you do not come, my life will stand still. I will drown in the ocean of my tears. Krishna! As the blade of grass longs to embrace the cloud, please pour down as the gentle rain.

rādhā bhāvam aṙiyill-ennālum
kṛṣṇā nin virahattil ñān tapippū
mādhavā madhuramām nin rūpamōrkkil
puḷakitam ākunnu arikil ettān – kṛṣṇā...

O Krishna, I know nothing of Radha's divine love, yet I suffer the pain of separation from you. O Madhava, remembering your sweet form, I yearn to come close to You.

kaṇṇane kāṇān uzhaṙunna kaṇṇilum
muraḷika kēḷkkān vembunna kātilum
śrīdharā! hṛttilum viḷaṅgīṭaṇē sadā
ninnilāy ennum ñān layicciṭaṭṭe – kṛṣṇā.

Sridhara! O consort of Lakshmi, illumine my heart and my eyes and ears that long to see and hear you. May I merge in you forever.

laḷitāmbikē ammē (Malayalam)

laḷitāmbikē ammē amṛtāmbikē
praṇamikkunnu ñān lōkamātē
ninde taṇalil vaḷarttīṭaṇē
sarva śaktē ende ammē

O Mother, beautiful goddess, mother of immortality, I bow down before you, mother of the world. Please make me grow in Your shade, my mother, all powerful one!

tava pādāmbujam tēṭi aṇayum
bhṛṅgaṅgaḷ ākaṭṭe en mizhikaḷ
ā madhumādhuryam nukarnnu ñānum
unmattabhāvattil āṇḍiṭaṭṭe
ammē...

May my eyes, like honey-bees, search for you. May I reach your lotus feet. Sipping that sweet nectar, may I dive into your euphoric bliss, O Mother.

mama hṛdayam tava śrīpuram ākaṭṭe
cintāmalar ñān arccikkaṭṭe
'amma' ennuḷḷa mantram japiccennum
ninnil layikkaṭṭe ende janmam
ammē

May my heart be your sacred shrine, and may I worship you with the flowers of my thoughts. Continuously chanting the mantra 'Amma,' may my life merge in You, O Mother.

Lämmössä tuulen (Finnish)

Lämmössä tuulen henkäyksen
Edessä luonnon kauneuden
Jokainen hetki mä olla saan
Sylissä äiti maan

In the warmth of the wind's breath, before nature's beauty, every single moment I'm fortunate to be in the arms of mother earth.

Kirkkaana yönä tähdet ja kuu
Seuraavat kun häly vaimentuu
Hiljennyn rauhaan valtavaan
Sylissä äiti maan

On a clear night, the stars and the moon witness the noise subside. I withdraw into the immense silence in the arms of mother earth.

Auringon loiste mittaamaton
Syvällä minunkin sielussa on
Kytkeydyn voimaan valtavaan
Sylissä äiti maan

The unlimited effulgence of the sun resides deep in my soul. I connect to unlimited power in the arms of mother earth.

Myrskyinen matka elämä on
Sydän on rikki ja onneton
Satama löytyy ainoastaan
Sylissä äiti maan

Life is a stormy ride of broken hearts and unhappiness. The only safe haven is in the arms of mother earth.

Liebe Amma (German)

Liebe Amma bitte gib uns Gnade
Diese grosse Welt braucht deine Gnade

Dear Amma, please give us grace. This vast world needs Your grace!

Jay ma Ambe Durge ma Jay ma Devi Kali ma
Gnade Gnade über alles Gnade

Victory to Mother Durga, Mother Devi and Mother Kali. Grace, grace, above everything, grace!

Liefde voor God (Dutch)

Liefde voor God, onze ware natuur,
oneindig bewustzijn, een hart zo puur
Gedachten verhind'ren, als 'n wolk voor de zon
het stralende licht, de innerlijke bron

Love for God, our own true nature, infinite consciousness, a heart so pure. Like a cloud before the sun, thoughts conceal the radiant light, the inner source

Amma, help te vertrouwen, dat 't ik oplossen zal
en zó de weg vrijkomt, naar 't eeuwige al

O Amma, help me to trust that the 'I' will dissolve, that the way to eternal wholeness will be cleared.

Hoe lang nog de strijd, van hoofd en hart,
buigen en schouwen, tot de geest is ontward
Laat stílte spreken en zíe wie je bent,
De opdracht dit leven, dat 't zèlf wordt gekend

How much longer the struggle, between head and heart. I bow down and watch until my mind is clear. Let silence speak to reveal who you are. The goal of life is to know the Self.

Alleen mèt Gods genade keert de eenheid terug,
in besef van de Waarheid, bent U de brug

Only by God's grace is Oneness revealed. By knowing the Truth, you build the bridge.

Amma Amma Amma Amma

Llum de la llum (Catalan)

Llum de la Llum, Mare del Món
Llum del meu cor, Amor refulgent
Llum de la Llum, Presència infinita
Mare tan sols Tu, Mare tan sols Tu

Light of the light, Mother of the world, light of my heart, effulgent love. Light of the light, infinite presence. Mother only You, Mother only You!

Els dies passen, s'escola el temps
He de trobar-te, digue'm on ets
Soc al teu cor, mira al revés
Estic més a prop que tu mateix.

Days go by, time slips away, I must find You. Tell me, where are You? I'm in your heart, look inward. I'm closer to you than you are to yourself.

Amma, Amma, Amma, Amma...

Mirada clara i un cor innocent
Un somriure als llavis i al pensament

Una mà que ajuda sense esperar res,
I em podràs veure a tot arreu.

A clear gaze, an innocent heart, a smile on your lips and in your mind. Give a helping hand without any expectations, and you will see Me everywhere.

Love is you, love is me (English)

Love is you, love is me.
Love is far beyond what you can see.
Love is warm and gives relief

in a smile in your eyes.
All the beauty is not enough.
Love cannot be described.

Love, love, love, love --
Love is the only answer.
All the paths begin and end in love.

Love love love love--
Words can't give you sweetness
of the universal language of love.

Love love love love--
In love there are no concepts.
Love destroys the 'you and me'
for 'one, eternal one'.

Love love love love--
Don't be afraid of darkness.
Let's light the lamp of hope and love.

Keep the lamp light on in your heart.

Lurreko mantu leuna (Basque)

Lurreko mantu leuna
Zure besarkada laztana
Hor bota bihotzean gordetako
malkoak eta pozak.

Your darling embrace is Mother Earth´s cloak of sweet protection. In Your darling embrace I cry the tears and joys stored in my heart.

Ammatxu maitea, Ammatxu maitea,
Ammatxu maitea, Zure
seme-alabak zaintzen dozuna...

The beloved divine Mother takes care of Her child.

Gure negu-gorrietan
Zure oin kutunetan
lagatzen doguz bizi honetako
nekeak eta ametsak.

In it barren winters, we leave the efforts and hopes for our life at Your dear feet.

Maadare man (Persian)

Maadare man
Ey khodaye man
Man ghomshode-am
To kojaa-asti

My mother, O my God! I am lost, where are you?

Ba biigonayi
dombaalee to raftam
Dar dasht o biiyaban
dombalee to gashtam

With innocence, I set out to find you. In the plains and deserts, I have searched for you.

Ba pahaye shekaste
Va vojude khaste
Bego man alan
Be kojaa residam?

With broken feet and a tired soul, tell me where have I reached now?

Hezaaran baare
To ra faryaad zadam
Chera man ra aslan
To nemishnavi?

Thousands of times I've called you. Why can't you hear me?

Ba hame darda
Hanoz omid daram

Midonam ke rozi
Be daadam miressi

With all my hurts, I still have faith that one day you will answer my call.

Khodaa
Ey khodaa
Ey khodye man
Ey khodye man

God, O God, O my God!

Mā inspire l'amour (French)

Mā inspire l'amour
Ōm expire la lumière
La respiration est une rivière
qui nous relie à toi

Ma, inhale love. Om, exhale light. Our breath is a river that connects us to You.

Sur la rivière de mon souffle
guidés par la lumière
L'amour est le chemin
qui nous conduit au divin

On the river of my breath, I am led by light. Love is the path that leads us to the divine.

Sur la rivière de mon souffle
Amma tu es là

Tu nous ouvres grand les bras
qu'enfin nous plongions en Toi

On the river of my breath, You are there, Amma. You open Your arms wide for us, that, at last, we may dive into You.

Mā... ōm... mā... ōm...

Mā kālī devī (French)

Ma Kali, Dévi,
Ô Mère je me languis
De ton divin chant,
Toi qui offres à ma vie,
L'éternel présent.

My Mother Kali, Devi, I long for your divine song. You gift my life with the eternal present.

Le son de ta voix
Guide mes pas,
Je vibre de ta joie.
Divine mélodie,
De ma sombre Kali.

The sound of Your voice guides my steps. I vibrate with your joy. Divine melody, of my dark Kali.

Ma Kali Devi... Ma Kali Devi...

Et mon âme éblouie
Contemple infinie,
La roue de toute vie
Surgit de l'oubli

And my dazzled soul contemplates, infinitely, the wheel of all life arising from oblivion.

Et j'entends ta voie,
Puissante et claire
Qui d'amour me foudroie
Douceur infinie
De ma sombre Kali

I hear Your voice, powerful and clear, striking me with love. Infinite sweetness of my dark Kali.

Et je chante en ma nuit
Le nom de Kali
Au rythme de sa danse,
Éternel silence

I sing Kali's name in my night, to the rhythm of Her dance, eternal silence.

Et je suis ta voie,
O délivrance,
Pleurant des larmes de joie
Divine mélodie
de ma sombre Kali

I follow Your path, O deliverance, crying tears of joy. Divine melody of my dark Kali.

manasē ō manasē (Kannada)

manasē ō manasē svīkarisu
elladakku sammatisu

O mind, accept all and consent to all.

nagē bandāgā ēkendu keḷu vadillā
sukhabandāgā ēkemba praśnē illā
aḷu bandāgā ēkendu kēḷuvē
duḥkha bandāgā ēkendu kēḷuvē

When life brings laughter we never ask, 'Why?' When it brings happiness, we never question it. When it brings tears, we ask, "Why?" When it brings sorrow we ask, "Why?"

manasē manasē ō
gurupadakamalam smarahṛdi satatam

O mind, O mind, constantly remember the Guru's lotus feet in your heart!

geḷuvu bandāgā ēkendu kēḷu vadillā
sōlu bandāgā ēkendu kēḷuvē
huṭṭibandāgā ēkemba praśnē illā
sāvu bandāgā idēnemba kēḷvē

When life brings victory we never ask, "Why?" When it brings defeat, we ask, "Why?" When we are born, we never question it. When death arrives we ask, "What is this?"

svīkarisu ellavanu svīkarisu
śaraṇāgu śaraṇāgu guruvina pādakē śaraṇāgu

Accept. Just accept everything. Surrender, surrender, surrender to the feet of the Guru.

manassil menayunna (Malayalam)

manassil menayunna māyā citraṅgaḷ
māyāte maṙayāte nilkkum
maraṇam māṭi viḷikkunna nērattum
manujan maṙakkān maṭikkum

The fantasies in our mind remain indelible. Even when death calls, we are reluctant to forget about them.

mananam ceytīṭukil manam-aṙiññīṭukil
mānasam maunamāy tīrum
mati teḷiññīṭilō mizhi tuṙakkum - marttyan
palatum maṙakkān paṭhikkum

If we reflect on and understand our mind, it will fall silent. As the intellect becomes clear, we gain insight and learn to forget many of the things we cherished.

mātāvin maṭi tannil mukham cāyukil - manam
mādhurya nirbharamākum
madhu atu nukarilō manamaṭaṅgum - maraṇa
-bhayameṅgō pōy maṙaññīṭum

If we rest our head in Mother's lap, our mind will be filled with sweetness. Savoring that bliss subdues our mind and the fear of death vanishes.

manavē kāraṇa (Kannada)

manavē kāraṇa bandhanake
manavē kāraṇa mōkṣake
yamaniyamagaḷa pālipaśiṣyage
bandhana biḍugaḍe mārgava tōralu
avatarisiruvaru jagadoḷage... guru jagadoḷage...
ī jagadoḷage

Our mind is the cause of both bondage and liberation. For the disciple who follows yama and niyama (do's and don'ts), the guru has incarnated on this earth to show the path from bondage to liberation.

bhagavadgītaya abhyasisalu
sadguruvina jīvana nidarśana
nija darśanavu... nija darśanavu... nija darśanavu
ariṣṭu vargava toredu jīvisalu
karma jñāna bhakti yōgagaḷu

The sadguru's life itself is the teachings of the Bhagavad Gita. The sadguru's life teaches the disciple how to live a life devoid of the arishadvargas (the six enemies of the mind). The guru guides the disciple to practice karma, jñana and bhakti yogas.

cittaśuddhiyim sthitaprajñayim
nirahamkāradi śāntiya honduta
guruvina pādada mahime indalē
aikyanāguvanu hariyoḷage
śrīhariyoḷage... śrīhariyoḷage
guru ōm hari ōm...

Through purifying the mind, being steadfast and equanimous in all circumstances, and being egoless, the disciple attains eternal peace. He merges in Sreehari only by the glory of the feet of the sadguru.

mā śakti hai (Punjabi)

mā śakti hai... mā bhakti hai... mā mukti hai...
mā śakti hai mā bhakti hai
prēm dā dīp jalāyā hai

Mother is energy. Mother is devotion. Mother is liberation. She has lit the lamp of love.

kāl dē cakar to bāhar... ō...
mukti dvār dikhāyā hai
mukti dvār dikhāyā hai
mukti dvār dikhāyā hai

From the wheel of time, She shows us the door to liberation.

muskān tēri ne ō mā
sūraj can camkāyā hai
akhā band jā khuliyā hō
rūp tērā darśāyā hai

Your smile has the radiance of the sun. Whether my eyes are closed or open, You have revealed Your form.

śānti dā sandēś phelāo
jay mā jay mā gānde jāō

Spread the message of peace. Singing, 'Victory to Mother!'

rake jithe tū kadam ō mā
kamalā dā bāg khiḍāyā hai
dey vī khuṣbū hai har pāse... ō....
madōṣi nū jagāyā hai

Wherever Your holy feet walk, a garden of lotuses blooms. Their fragrance everywhere causes divine intoxication.

tēriyā bāhā ne ō mā
sansār nū samāyā hai
prēm tērē ne patthar nū vi
mōm vāng pighalāyā hai

In Your arms, O Mother, the world is absorbed. In Your love, even a stone melts like wax.

māyai adu niṙaindirukkum (Tamil)

māyai adu niṙaindirukkum
māya ulagam tāyē
unnai viṭṭagandragandru
nāḷum nānum senṭrēn tāyē

In this world full of illusion, day after day, I kept wandering away from You.

māyai adan pinnē sellum
undan siṙu kuzhandai amma
pala muṙai vizhundu aṭippaṭṭālum
vāzhvin nōkkam aṙiyāmal vāzhkiṙēn

Amma, I am your little baby who runs after the illusory objects of the world. I have fallen many times, but still I have not understood the goal of life.

azhagu oḷirum tāyē
akhilattai kāppāy nīyē
aṙavaṇaittem vāzhvil āṙudal tandu
ulakirkku udavum uḷḷam taruvāy

Mother of dazzling beauty, please protect the world. Please embrace us and comfort us. Grant us the mind to be helpful to the world

ippiṙappum eppiṙappum
nīyē endan aḍaikkalam
bhaktiyum śaktiyum tandu ennai
kaippiḍittu sella vēṇḍum amma

You are my sole refuge in this birth and in every birth. Amma, give me devotion, give me strength. Hold my hand and lead the way!

Mir, lyubov' (Russian)

Mir, lyubov', krasata
Prabuzh dayetsya Mater' Zemlya
Mir, lyubov', krasata
Prabuzh dayutsya nashi serdtsa

Peace, love, beauty—Mother Earth awakens. Peace, love, beauty—our hearts are awakening.

Krasatoy lyubvi i garmoniyey
Razukrasili muy nebesa

Nebesa apustilis'na Zemlyu
VRayskiysad prevratilas' Ana

With the beauty of love and harmony, we painted heaven. Heaven came down to Earth and became the Garden of Eden.

Chistym svetom siyayet planeta
Plamya istiny yarka garit
Svet-lyubov' pashol atavsyudoo
My vernulis' v prastranstvo lyubvi

The planet shines with pure light. The flame of Truth burns bright. The light of love shines from everywhere. We returned to the place of love.

O, Akian Lyubvi,
Kaplyu svayu primi
Pazvol' mne slit' sya sta boy
Vernoot' syak sebe damoy

O ocean of love, receive this little drop. Let me merge into You. Let me return home.

Mother divine (English)

Mother divine, pure love in us all,
Mother divine pure love in us all.

How many lifetimes
lost in the forest of our dreams,
chasing our shadow,
missing the bliss of our true being, our true being.

Catch the hem of Her sari
as Kali dances and twirls.
Find that She alone
has become this whole world, this whole world.

In every face, discover the trace of divinity.
Find Her shining
in every person that you see,
all that you see.

jay mā... jay jay mā
jay mā... jay jay mā

Mother ocean (English)

Mother ocean, let me leap
into your love. Take me deep
beyond wave and shore
where division is no more.

I set out for a pearl
but got lost in the world.
Take me now, rescue me.
May your love set me free.
Show me what life is worth
in the goal of life on earth.

As my past and my dreams
wash away, love redeems.
Let me merge into you,

ocean pure crystal blue.
Chanting 'ma', chanting 'om'
carry me, bring me home.

ma... om...

Moye serce byotsya (Russian)

Мое сердце бьётся чаще, в ней я вижу солнца свет,
Рядом с ней все стало ярче, словно чувств моих рассвет.

Moye serce byotsya chashche, v ney ya vizhu sonca svet,
Ryadom s ney vse stalo yarche, slovno chustf moih rasvet.

My heart beats faster. In her I see the sun light. Next to her everything became brighter. My feelings awakened like the sunrise

Краски ярко заиграли, вдруг почувствовал любовь,
Об одном прошу тебя я, посмотри на меня вновь.

Kraski yarko zaigrali, vdrug pochustvoval lyubov,
Ob odnom proshu tebya ya, posmotri na menya vnov.

The colors began to play brightly. Then, suddenly, I felt love. I ask you about one thing. Look at me again.

Взгляд твой теплый и открытый
переполненный любви
Амма, сердце замирает, от твоей к нам
доброты.

Vzglyat tvoy tepliy i otkrytiy perepolnenniy lyubvi
Amma, serce zamirayet, ot tvoyey k nam dobroty.

Amma, your warm and open gaze overflows with love. My heart stops from your kindness.

То тепло, что ты нам даришь, пронесём через
года,
Мама, Мама, Амма, Амма, в нашем сердце
навсегда.

To teplo, shto ty nam darish, pronesyom cherez
goda,
Mama, Mama, Amma, Amma, v nashem serce
nafsegda.

The warmth that you give will stay with us for years. Mother, mother, Amma Amma in our hearts forever.

Повстречав тебя однажды, вслед пошел я не
спеша,
Как же ты прекрасна Мама, как душа твоя
нежна.

Povstrechav tebya odnazhdy, vsled poshel ya ne
spesha,

Kak zhe ty prekrasna Mama, kak dusha tvoya nezhna.

Meeting you once, I started following you slowly. How beautiful you are, Mother, how tender is your soul

Все мы дети в этом мире, ты ведёшь нас за собой
Смело мы вперед шагаем, когда слышим голос твой

Vse my deti v etom mire, ty vedyosh nas za soboy
Smelo my vpered shagayem, kogda slishim golos tvoy

We are all your children in this world. You are leading us. We step out braver when we hear your voice.

То тепло, что ты нам даришь, пронесём через года,
Мама, Мама, Амма, Амма, в нашем сердце навсегда

To teplo, shto ty nam darish, pronesyom cherez goda,
Mama, Mama, Amma, Amma, v nashem serce nafsegda

The warmth that you give us, we will carry through the years. Amma, Amma, Amma, Amma, in our heart forever.

mṛtyuñjaya hara (Sanskrit)

mṛtyuñjaya hara śambhō śaṅkara
pārvati śaṅkara girijā śaṅkara

O great Lord Shiva, Shankara, conqueror of death, consort of goddess Parvati who was born from the mountain!

jaḍājūṭadhara tējōvigraha
candrakalādhara jaya gaṅgādhara
trayambakēśvara mahāyōgīśvara
pāpavināśaka parama dayākara

You have matted locks and Your form is resplendent. You are the three-eyed Rudra, and the great lord of the yogis. You destroy sin and are supremely merciful.

hālāhaladhara nīlakaṇṭha śiva
nāgahāradhara bhasma vibhūṣita
vyāghrāmbaradhara jaya abhayaṅkara
praṇava svarūpā pāvana caraṇā

O Shiva, your throat turned blue when You held the halahala poison. You are adorned with snakes and smeared with ash. Victory to You who wear a tiger skin and bestow fearlessness! You are the very nature of the syllable Om, and Your feet are pure.

śiva śiva śivāya śivāya namaḥ ōm
hara hara harāya harāya namaḥ ōm
śivāya namḥ ōm harāya namaḥ ōm
bhavabhaya harāya harāya namaḥ ōm

Salutations to Lord Shiva, salutations to Lord Hara, you who destroy the fear of transmigration!

muḷam taṇḍil (Malayalam)

muḷam taṇḍil ozhuki varum
vēṇugāna madhurimaykkāy
kāttirippū rādha ennum
ninnil-aṇayānāy nī
ennil aliyānāy

Radha is waiting to hear the sweet song flow from your flute, to reach you and to merge in you.

mānatte candrika tan
pāloḷippuñciri kāṇke
mānasattil mādhavanum
puñciri tūki naṙum
puñciri tūki

The moon smiled at Radha from the sky. In her mind, Madhavan also smiled radiantly.

mōha yavanika nīṅgi māṙi
mōhanan tan vēṇugānam
mōdamōḍe mānasattil
malar niṙaccu veṇ
malar niṙaccu

The veil of delusion fell from her mind. The song of my sweet Lord flooded her mind with bliss and blossomed as flowers.

maṙannuvō rādha ennum
endētu mātramennu
ōtiyende kātukaḷil

ārum aṙiyāte nī
ārum aṙiyāte

Has Radha forgotten that Krishna whispered secretly in her ear: "You are mine and mine alone."

muruga muruga (Malayalam)

muruga muruga skanda guru nāthā
muruga muruga skanda guru nāthā

vivēcanādhikāram nēṭunnatin
śivagiri kunnil tapassu ceytu kumaran

Murugan performed penance on top of the Shivagiri mountain to gain the power to discriminate between the transient and the eternal.

ajñatayuṭe andhakāram
manuṣya manassine valayam ceytu

The darkness of ignorance has filled the human mind.

ajñatakketire pōrāṭān nām
jñānattinde yōddhākkaḷ ākaṇam

To combat ignorance, may we become warriors of knowledge!

jñānattinde yōddhākkaḷ ākān
subrahmaṇya svāmi nī anugrahikku

O Lord Subrahmanya, please bless us to become warriors of knowledge!

subrahmaṇya svāmi nin kṛpa ēki
ñaṅgaḷuṭe prārthana svīkarikku

Lord Subrahmanya, please bestow Your grace, and accept our prayer!

harō harā harō harā, skanda guru nāthā

nā kaṇṭiki velugu (Telugu)

nā kaṇṭiki velugu nīvammā
nī callani cūpē cālammā

You are the light in my eyes, Amma. One soothing look from you is enough for me, Amma.

oka nīyani māṭē ammā
anurāgāniki arttham ammā

One sweet word from you is enough for me, Amma. You are the meaning of affection, Amma.

mamakāraniki mūlam ammā
sahanāniki tīram ammā

You are the source of love, Amma. You are the shore of patience, Amma!

dēvuḍu pampina rūpam ammā
kadilē dēvata nīvammā

You are the God-sent form, Amma. You are the moving goddess, Amma!

Nakhtalifu (Arabic-Egyptian)

Nakhtalifu fil lisaan
Nakhtalifu fil alwaan
Nakhtalifu fil afkaar
Nakhtalifu fil adyaan
Lakin Ilahuna saabit

Rabbul bachar waahed
Fi hubbihi najtami'uu
wa kulluna insaan

Our languages, colors, ideas and religions differ; but our God is fixed. The lord of humankind is One. In His love we meet, and we are all human beings.

La taghlibukal humuum
Wanzur ilal tuyuur
alya'su laysa lahu makaanun
tatiiru fawkal ghuyuum
Maa'una elilaah shaahed
Rabbul bachar waahed
Fi hubbihi najtaami'uu
wa kulluna insaan

Don't let worries overcome you. Look at the birds. Despair has no place with them. They fly over the clouds. God watches over us. The lord of humankind is One. In His love we meet, and we are all human beings.

Ih'lam bil salaam
walhubbu walwiaam
La tastasni ahadun
min ayyil anaam
fa ilaahuna maajed
Rabbul bachar waahed
Fi hubbihi najtami'uu
wa kulluna insaan

Dream of peace, love and harmony. Don't exclude anyone from God's creation. Our God is generous. The lord of humankind is One. In His love we meet, and we are all human beings.

in ataabatka lhuruub
ta'ammal fil malakuut
tajiddul hakikata jaliiya
fal hubbub la yamuut
fa ilahuunal salaam
Rabbul bachar waahed
Fi hubbihi najtami'uu
wa kulluna insaan

If you're tired of wars, meditate on the universe. You'll find the clear Truth that love never dies. Our God is peace. The lord of humankind is One. In His love we meet, and we are all human beings.

nalvazhikāṭṭiṭu jayalakṣmi (Tamil)

nalvazhi kāṭṭiṭu jayalakṣmi
śaktiyai tandiṭu nārāyaṇi

Show me the right path, O Jayalakshmi! (Goddess of victory and conquering hurdles). Grant me strength, O Narayani! (representation of Devi as Lord Vishnu's sister)

aṇuvāka nī irundum unnai uṇaravillai
tirukkōvil sannidhiyil unaikkāṇavillai
idayattil vasikkinṭrāy ena nānum arindēn
ennuḷḷē nīyum vasikkinḍrāyō?

Though You dwell in every cell and atom, I have not realized Your presence. I have not seen you in a temple shrine. I have come to know that you reside in our hearts. Does that mean you reside within me too?

enkenku kaṇḍālum kāṭciyellām
sōdanaikaḷ vēdanaikaḷ sōgaṅkaḷē
ānālum ennuḷḷē nīyirukka
enakkenna kavalai dēviyammā

Wherever I look, I see only trials and tribulations, pain and despair. But you are within me at all times, so what should I worry about?

ennuḷḷē alaipāyum māyaiyenum kaṭalin
kalaṅkarai viḷakkamāy nīviḷaṅkināyē
un pādam paṇindiṭa kāḷi ennai nī
karam piṭittu karai sērttu kāttiṭuvāy

As I drown in the ocean of samsara and maya, you are the lighthouse that brightens my path. O Kali, grab hold of me and pull me ashore, that I may fall at Your holy feet!

ñān aṙiyunnu (Malayalam)

ñān aṙiyunnu ānandamē
nī tanne ñān enna nitya satyam
māṙunna lōkattil māṙunnu ñānum
māṙātta ninne maṙann-ammē – ammē

O blissful one, I know the eternal Truth that I am one with You. I also undergo change in this changing world, and I forget you, the changeless one. O Mother!

raṇḍenna bhāvattil uṇarunna duritaṅgaḷ
onnenna bhāvattil amarumallō

saccidānandam-en ātmasvarūpam
nityātma bōdhattil uṇarunna satyam

The difficulties that spring from seeing duality will disappear when I see Oneness. Let me know that my true nature is sat, chit and ananda (existence consciousness bliss), awareness, atma.

ātma-svarūpavum prēma-svarūpavum
nī tanne martyā maṙanniṭallē
paramārttha tattvam-itaṙiññiṭāte
ī janmam veṙute pōkkiṭallē

O Man, remember that you are of the nature of the atma, the embodiment of love. Do not waste your life. Know this supreme Truth.

nin malarvāṭiyil (Malayalam)

nin malarvāṭiyil oru ceru pūvāy
viṭarān vembunna malar moṭṭu ñān
āśakaḷ neytu mōhaṅgaḷ neytu
nin malar vāṭiyil tattikkaḷikkān

I am a tiny bud that longs to bloom in your garden. I dream dreams and hope and long to sway in the gentle breeze.

naru nilāvinde ī ponprabhayil
ānanda mattanāyi ñān āṭavē
iruḷin agādhatakkuḷḷil ninnu
oru ceru nōvennil paṭarnniraṅgi
ammā ammā
oru ceru nōvennil paṭarnniraṅgi

As I sway, intoxicated in the radiance of the moonlit night, from the depths of darkness, a tiny sorrow spread through me. O Mother, a tiny sorrow spread through me.

en manō vēdana eṅgum paṭaravē
nin kaitiriveṭṭam ennil teḷiññu
nin snēhadhārayām kāruṇyam illāykil
ī pulariyil ñān illayammē! ammā ammā
ī pulariyil ñān illayammē!

As the pain in my heart overcame me, your luminous light became clear within. If the stream of your compassion had not washed over me, I would not have greeted the morning, O Mother! I would not be here this morning.

ninnapāda sēvēmāḍalū (Kannada)

ninnapāda sēvēmāḍalū bandihēnammā
bhavabādhē nīggisū bhavatāriṇi ammā

I came to serve at Your feet, O Mother. You who carry us across the ocean, protect me from the misery of samsara.

jarāmarā suḷiyallī silukiruva jīvikaḷā
mōhapāśadindā biḍisi uddharisu ammā
etta nōḍalattalū kēḷutihudu ārthanāda
maradēvana manadinenedu bhītagoṇḍiharu
ammā... ammā... ammā... ammā

Save the jivas from the delusions of the endless cycle of birth and death. Everywhere we look, jivas are lost in the illusory world. Caught by the noose of Yama, everyone is suffering.

Release me from the noose of attachment and uplift me. I hear sounds of misery everywhere.

prakṛti kṣīṇagoḷḷuttidē layasūccanē mūḍidde
yellarāsē mitimīrī adharmmavē heccidē
avatārarūpi ammā ninagidō namanavu
jagadi śāndi pasarisi yellarā rakṣisu

Nature is disturbed and hints that dissolution is near. Desire has gone beyond limits, and adharma is increasing. Salutations to you, Avatari Amma. You spread peace in the world. Please uplift everyone!

ninna makkaḷellarannu hṛdayakkē āṇissi
prēma karuṇāmṛtada dhāreyā harisu
śānti samādhāna yellarigu sigalendu
paramārttha jñānava bōdhisu ō tāyē

Hugging all Your children, shower love and compassion on them. We pray that all find peace and tranquility. Please impart true knowledge.

nin pādapadmattil aṇayān (Malayalam)

nin pādapadmattil aṇayān kotikkē
en manō mālinya timiram marayāy
mara nīkki nin pāda malarukaḷ pulkuvān
aruḷaṇē nin kṛpa aṭiyanil ennum

Even when I come close to your lotus feet, mental impurities cloud my vision. Please bless me with your grace and remove this veil that I may forever embrace your lotus feet.

nin divya sannidhiyil aṇayuvānāyi
ennile lōkāśa māttaṇē dēvi
ninne ariññiṭān ninnil aliññiṭān
nin kṛpa ennilāy coriyaṇē dēvi

O Devi, please remove my desire for the world, that I may reach your divine presence. Please shower your grace on me, Devi, that I may know you and merge in you.

ammē... ammē... ammē
hṛdayēśvari jagadīśvari

O Mother! Goddess of my heart, goddess of the world...

nin rūpam ennum en uḷḷil teḷiyān
nin nāmam ennum en cuṇḍil viṭarān
ninnaruḷ vacanaṅgaḷ kātil muzhaṅgān
nin kṛpa ennilāy coriyaṇē dēvi

For your form to shine always within, for your name to blossom on my lips, for your blessed words to resonate in my ears, O Devi, please shower your grace upon me!

nīr bharā (Hindi)

nīr bharā nayan hai, dard bharā dil hai
man māyā jāl meṅ, uljhā huā phir hai
tujhsē dūr na lē jāyē, pās mujhē lēlō mā
gōd mē tērī āj mujhē biṭhā lō mā, sambhālō mā

With tear-filled eyes and an aching heart, my mind is ensnared by this illusory world. Don't let it tempt me away from you! Hold me close, take me in Your lap and save me, Mother!

raṅg bhari duniyā ki ḍōr
khīñcē mujhē apnī aur
ḍūb na jāūṅ sansār mēṅ
jaldi lēlō bāhōṅ mēṅ

Due to my ignorance, I chase after this distracting world. O Mother, quickly take me in Your arms and save me from drowning!

mā... jay jay mā... mā... mēri mā...

viśva śakti sañcālini mā
mukti mārg vidhāyini mā
jānē añjānē hūi bhūlōṅ kō
kṣamā karō vardāyini mā

You are the power of the universe, the only one who can guide us. Please forgive the mistakes I have committed, knowingly or unknowingly.

niṣphala-svapnattil (Malayalam)

niṣphala-svapnattil muzhuki en nāḷukaḷ
ñān ariyāte kaṭannu pōyi
kramamatta cintā-pravāha-tirakaḷil
muṅgiyum poṅgiyum ñān kuzhaṅgi

The days pass by, and I remain immersed in vain dreams. Strong currents of disorderly thoughts confuse me and pull me down and throw me up.

sukhamām madhuvoru ceru-tuḷḷimōntavē
duritam-orāzhiyāy ārttirambī

sphaṭika-samānam-en svapnaṅgaḷ okkeyum
vidhiyuḍe tallētt-uṭaññupōyi

Even as I sip a drop of nectarine happiness, sorrow roars in like an ocean. My dreams lie shattered by the hands of fate.

uṇmaye-tēṭiyen mānasam-alayumbōḷ
vighnaṅgaḷil taṭṭi vīṇupōyi
duḥssahamām duḥkha-svapnaṅgaḷāl-uḷḷam
bhītiyāl kambitam-āyiṭunnu

My mind roams around seeking the Truth, but it beats against obstacles and falls down. My mind trembles in fear at unbearable nightmares.

rāppakal tāṇḍiyī kālam-akalumbōḷ
verum-oru prēkṣakan-āvunnu ñān
ennātma-bōdham uṇarumō ammē ñān
ennile enne ariññīṭumō?

Time passes with each day and night, and I am a mere spectator. Will my Self-awareness awaken, O Mother? Will I ever know the real Me within me?

nityānandattil (Malayalam)

nityānandattil nirantaram nilakoḷḷum
nityaprakāśam ennammē
nī maruvum-amōgha nirvṛtiyilēkk-enne
kaitāṅgi nayiccīṭukille

O my Mother! You are eternal radiance, ever established in immortal bliss. Please hold my hand and lead me to the exalted tranquility in which you abide!

divyamām jīvitōdyānattil ninnu nī
kēḷikaḷāṭi timirttīṭumbōḷ
tuccham ī śalyaka bhītiyil uzhaṙi ñān
ninnilēkk-aṇayāte pakaccu ninnu

You delight in your divine games in the garden of life, and I stand helpless in anxious fear, unable to turn inward and reach you.

tāyē puṇarnniṭān ōṭi varū
tāyē puṇarnniṭān vēgam varū

O Mother! Please come running to hug me. O Mother, please come fast to hug me!

ūzhiyil aihika cuzhiyil akapēṭṭu
pōyi innī pāvam ennambikē
nin padamalariṇa kaiviṭṭu pōkayil
jīvitam vyartthamām ennambikē

O Mother of the universe! I am caught in the whirlpool of worldly life. Dearest mother, if ever I let go of your lotus feet, my life will be in vain.

Noor a veen (Irish)

Noor a veen on greean ina lee
iss an dur-ka-dus chim-pil ur-in
Kweev-nee ern waher awr waher on graw

When the sun sleeps and darkness is all around, remember Mother, our Mother of love.

Been shee egg law-arch treej on nyaal-ak,
tree na raail-tee, treej-on greean sa spair.

She speaks through the moon, the stars, the sun in the sky.

Been she egg cahna linn, eg goy-ra linn,
egg dow-sa linn i go-o-o-nee
Marshin kahna ley-hee, goy-ra ley-hee,
dow-sa ley-hee i go-nee

She sings with us, laughs with us, dances with us, always. So let us sing with her, laugh with her, dance with her, always.

Iss ee on tol-av hees iss on spair hoos
Been she in-awr kree, maar graw du kawk

She is the earth below. She is the sky above. She is in our hearts as love for all.

jay ma jay ma jay ma jay ma
jay ma jay ma jay ma jay ma
jay ma jay ma jay ma jay ma

O Amma, please come (English)

O Amma, please come to me,
forgive me my mistakes.

You are my Kali.
You are my Devi.
You are my Lakshmi.
You are my Saraswati.

O Amma, give me devotion.
O Amma, give me happiness.

O Amma, grant me knowledge.
O Amma, grant me forgiveness.

O Amma, you are my God.
O Amma, you are my master.
O Amma, you are my love.
O Amma, you are my whole world.

amma amma kali amma
amma amma devi amma
amma amma durge amma
amma amma mate amma

Oh mind of mine (English)

Oh mind of mine,
selfishly blind,
surrender to the divine,
surrender to the divine.

From cradle to pyre, chasing your desires,
blindfolded you run, right into the fire.

Hold fast to this: the Truth exists!
It's name is eternal bliss.

All that you fear, for all that you pine,
all that is 'yours', all that is 'mine,'
all those you love, and those you disdain,
only this Truth is what shall remain.

Oi Äiti (Finnish)

Oi Äiti, kaipaus on luoksesi
kuuletko sydäntä?
Oi Äiti, ota minua kädestä!

O Mother, I miss being with you. Can you hear my heart? O Mother, please hold my hand?

Oi Äiti, olet valoni turvani, oikea onneni
Oi Äiti, olet rauha ja rakkaus, etsijän arvoitus

O Mother you are my light, my refuge, my real happiness. O Mother you are peace and love, the mystery to a seeker.

Devi Ma Devi Ma Devi Ma

Oi Äiti, suloinen ystävä, ihana iloni
Oi Äiti, tule mun luokseni!

O Mother you are my adorable friend, my sweet joy. O Mother, please come to me!

Oi Äiti, kiitos sun avusta, elämän onnesta
Oi Äiti, kiitos sanasta autuuteen, toivosta ikuiseen

O Mother, thank you for your help. Thank you for this life's joy. O Mother, thank you for the sacred word (mantra) that leads to eternal bliss. Thank you for the hope for eternity!

Devi Ma Devi Ma Devi Ma
Devi Ma Devi Ma

ō mā ō mā (Hindi)

ō mā... ō mā... ō mā... pyārī mā... (2)
lē lō śaraṇ mēṅ pyārī mā (2)
gyān kī jyōt jagā dō mā – mujhē
apnī śaraṇ mēṅ lēlō mā

O beloved Mother! O beloved Mother, grant me refuge. Awaken the flame of knowledge and give me refuge.

vāsanāōṅ sē muktī dilādō
sun kar mērī pukār ō mā – mujhē
apnī śaraṇ mēṅ lēlō mā

Hear to my call. Grant me freedom from negative tendencies and give me refuge.

janam janam sē bhaṭak rahī huṅ (2)
bhaktī kā pāṭh paḍhādō – mujhē
apnī śaraṇ mēṅ lēlō mā

Life after life, I wander lost. Show me the path of love, and grant me refuge.

ō mā kāḷī mā durgē mā pyārī mā
ō mā kāḷi mā durgē mā dēvi mā

O Beloved Mother Kali, O Durga!

ō mā sab lōkōṅ (Hindi)

ō mā sab lōkōṅ kī jananī
tērē caraṇōṅ kō maiṅ sumirūṅ

maiṅ tō bin pankhō kā panchī
tū dē kara-padmōṅ sē varadān

Mother of the universe, I contemplate Your holy feet. Being a wingless bird, please grant me a boon from Your lotus hands.

tērā dil karuṇā kī jaladhi
mērā man kartā hai binatī
ākē jaldī ab tū mujh kō
dēkē śaraṇ bacānā jananī

O fountain of compassion, my heart beseeches You. Come quickly and save me. Grant me refuge.

māyī sab pīḍāyēṅ har lē
sārē jag kī tū hē jananī
pāvē sab mā tērī karuṇā
nācō tum sārē vaibhav sē

O Mother of the universe, rid me of all my sorrows. Every being receives Your compassion. Dance, O Mother, in all Your glory and beneficence.

ōm namō bhagavatē rudrāya (Sanskrit)

ōm namō bhagavatē rudrāya
śiv śiv bhaj man, bhōlē nāth bhaj man

śiv śiv bhaj man, bhōlē nāth bhaj man
śambhō śaṅkara, śambhō śaṅkara śambhō
śaṅkara mahādēvā

sāmbasadāśiva sāmbasadāśiva sāmbasadāśiva
sāmbaśiva
sāmbasadāśiva sāmbaśiva

kāśikāpurādinātha jñānamuktidāyaka
tē namō namō namaḥ
tē namō namō namaḥ

bhaktavatsalāya śambhavē namō namō namaḥ
tē namo namō namaḥ
tē namo namō namaḥ

aṣṭasiddhidāyaka nīlakaṇṭha bhairava
manjunātha śaṅkarāya tē namō namō namaḥ

ḍam ḍam bhaj man har har bhaj man
ḍam ḍam bhaj man har har bhaj man
śambhō śaṅkara śambhō śaṅkara śambhō śaṅkara
mahādēva

sāmbasadāśiva sāmbasadāśiva sāmbasadāśiva
sāmbaśiva
har har bhōlēnāth kī (jay)

O my dear Kali (English)

O my dear Kali,
life is full of lessons.
If we learn them all
we surely will evolve.

O my dear Kali,
let my goal be mukti.
May I serve selflessly,
with sincerity.

O my dear Kali
obstacles are many.
Help me overcome them all
and, by your grace, I shall!

O my dear kali
trilokapālini
tripurasundari
tribhuvanēśvari

jai jai kāḷi mā jai jai kāḷi mā
jai jai kāḷi mā jai jai kāḷi mā

onnum uriyāṭān (Malayalam)

onnum uriyāṭān aṙiyāttorēzha ñān
prārtthanayō entennum-aṙiyilla
ammē nin munnil ñān veṙum oru pāvayō
calikkuvān pōlum ākātta paital ñān

I am a helpless one who does not even know how to pray. O Mother! I am only a puppet, a child sitting motionless before you.

collunnumilla en kadanaṅgaḷ ammē
vākkukaḷ nin munnil parimitamallō
enne ñān eṅgane ninnil arppikkum
arppikkuvān ñānuṇḍō nin munnil
arppikkuvān ñānuṇḍō nin munnil

O Mother! I am not telling you my sorrows. Words are of no use before you. How will I offer myself to you? But, am I really separate from you?

ñānilla ellām nīyennu ñān aṙiyumbōḷ
vākkukaḷ maṙayunnu cintakaḷ akalunnu
mānasakkaṭalin tirakaḷ aṭaṅgunnu
nīmātram ammē ī prapañcam ennaṙiyunnu
nīmātram ammē ī prapañcam ennaṙiyunnu

When I know that I am not real and you are everything, words fade away and thoughts disappear. The waves subside in the ocean of my mind. I realize that you are this manifest universe. I realize that you are this manifest universe.

oru mazhakkālavum (Malayalam)

oru mazhakkālavum vannu pōyi
manassinde maṙa nīkki
mazha-mukiloḷi varṇṇan
manatāril-ennu niṙaññu peyyum

Another monsoon has come and gone. When will my dark-hued Lord, the color of rain clouds, remove the veil from my heart? When will he pour down and revive my heart?

oru nṛtta-ccuvaṭinde gīti kēḷkkē
maṇināgatin mēlē
mazha-mukiloḷi-varṇṇan
maṇi-nṛttamāṭiyat-ōrttu ninnū

When I hear the rhythm of dancing steps, I remember my dark-hued Lord dancing on the hood of terrible Kaliya.

oru mayilppīli kaḷaññukiṭṭī
marataka kānti
kalarnna maṇirūpam
manatāril vannū niṙaññu ninnu

I found a peacock feather, and my mind became absorbed in the emerald beauty of my Lord.

orumātra nīyenne ōrttīṭumō
mārivil mānattu
māyāte nilkkumā
māsmara kāntiyāṇ-ende kaṇṇan

O Krishna! Will you remember me for even an instant? My Lord! You are the ever-fresh beauty that never fades in the rainbow sky.

oru nerippōṭ-eriyunnu (Malayalam)

oru nerippōṭ-eriyunn-antaraṅgē
jananī nī kaṇḍillennu naṭikkil
antaraṅgattile cintakaḷ ōrōnnum
aṙiyunna amma nī hṛdayēśvarī

O Mother! You pretend not to see the fire of longing that burns in my heart. Yet, O goddess of my heart, You know every thought of mine.

onnu tiriññu ñān nōkkumbōḷ ammē
ennum nīyenne nayicc-ennu kāṇunnu
ñān ariyāt-ende kūṭe naṭannu nī
ñān ariyāt-enne kāttīṭunnū

Mother! When I look back I realize that You have always led me. You walk beside me and protect me even though I am unaware of your presence.

satyamāyuḷḷ-oru snēhatte tēṭi ñān
janmāntaraṅgaḷ alaññirunnu
satyamāyuḷḷ-oru snēhamāṇ-īśvaran
eṅkil ā snēham enikk-ēkaṇē

For many lifetimes, I wandered in search of true love, O Mother! If indeed God is true love, then please bestow that love upon me.

īśvara-prēmattin vīcikaḷinn-ende
hṛttil niraññu kaviññiṭaṭṭe
niraññu kaviññ-ozhukunna prēmattinde
ādhāramāṇ-amma amṛtēśvarī

May my heart overflow with the waves of God's love. My Mother, Amriteshwari, is the very source of that overflowing divine love.

ā prēma-vānil paṙannu kaḷiccu ñān
ānanda unmattayāyīṭaṇē
ā prēma-vānilēkkinnu kutikkuvān
en manam vembunnu jagadambikē

May I be intoxicated with bliss, and fly and frolic in the sky of that divine love. O Mother! My heart longs to leap to that sky of love!

oru piñcupaitalām (Malayalam)

oru piñcupaitalām ennuḍe nombaram
aṙiyāttatentu nī ammē
ninnuḍe viḷikēḷkkān kātōrttirippū ñān
arikil aṇayāttat-entē... ammē

O Mother! Why do you not know the longing in the heart of your child. I wait for your call. Why are you not coming to me?

bhūlōkamātāvām amṛtēśvari ammē
aṙivinde poruḷākum ammē
aṙivillāt-uzhalunna agati tan akatāril
amarunnat-ennu nī ammē

O Mother Amriteswari, the Goddess of this universe, You are the essence of knowledge. When will you reside in the heart of this ignorant one?

māyatan sāgara-ccuzhiyil alayumbōḷ
āśrayam nīyē ammē
ānanda-dāyikē āśrita-vatsalē
nin pāda-padmattil cērkkukenne
tṛppāda-padmattil cērkkukenne

O Mother! You are my refuge when I am caught in the whirlpool of illusion. You are compassionate towards your devotees and the giver of bliss. Please merge me into your divine feet. May I merge into your lotus feet!

Ote bondie (Kreole)

Ote bondie a koz ou agarde pa moin
Mi attend aou vien a kote moin

Oh Amma! Why are You not looking at me? I am waiting for You to come near me.

Ziska kel her mi pler mon tou sel
Dan mon vi c ou mala bezoin
Kou done a moin out grace out lamour

How long will you let me cry alone? I need only You in my life. Please give me Your grace and Your love.

Jai Jai Kali Amma Kali

Ote bondie a genou mi mand a ou
Coup mon tet met otour out cou

Oh Amma! I beg You to remove my ego!

Faisak ou ve me largue pa mon main
Guide a moin si le bon somin
Apaiz mon ker, Apaiz mon douler

Do whatever You want with me, but never let go of my hand. Guide me in the right path. Comfort my heart, soothe my pain!

pāhimām pāhimām (Sanskrit)

pāhimām pāhimām jaganmātē pāhimām
viṣṇupatni pāhimām śrīlakṣmi dēvi pāhimām

mahālakṣmi varalakṣmi vīralakṣmi pāhimām
vēda purāṇētihāsa supūjita aṣṭalakṣmi pāhimām

Protect me, O mother of the universe, O Lakshmi, consort of Vishnu. O Mahalakshmi, giver of boons, give me courage! May the eight Lakshmis, worshipped in the Vedas, Puranas and Itihasas (scriptures), protect me!

ādilakṣmi mōkṣadāyini śāntiyutē pāhimām
dhānyalakṣmi mantra mūrtē padmanilayē pāhimām
dhairyalakṣmi bhārgavi śrī vaiṣṇavi mā pāhimām
gajalakṣmi śāstramayē saguṇavarṣiṇi pāhimām

O first among the Lakshmis, bestower of liberation and peace, goddess of grains (food), the embodiment of mantra, please protect me! Protect me, O Dhairyalakshmi (Lakshmi of courage), Bhargavi, Sri Vaishnavi! Gajalakshmi (goddess of elephants), who are well versed in scriptures and who bestow good qualities, please protect me!

santānalakṣmi hāsyamukhē lōkamātē pāhimām
vijayalakṣmi śaktidāyini vēdanutē pāhimām
vidyālakṣmi jñānamayē bhāratiśrī pāhimām
dhanalakṣmi ratnamayē bhāgyadāyini pāhimām

Eternal Lakshmi, you with a smiling face, please protect me. O goddess of victory, giver of strength, you who are extolled in Vedas, protect me! Goddess of knowledge, full of wisdom, the wealth of Bharat, protect me! O goddess of wealth, most invaluable gemstone, bestower of good fortune, protect me!

aṣṭalakṣmi pāhimām amṛtalakṣmi pāhimām

May the eight Lakshmis protect me. O Lakshmi of divine nectar, protect me!

pañcākṣara mandirattai (Tamil)

ninai keñjippāṭinān maṇivāsagan
koñjippāṭinān jñānasambandan
nañjippāḍinān nāvukkarasan
viñjippāḍinān azhagu sundaran

The ancient Tamil poets, Manikavachagar, Jnanasambandar, Tirunavukkarasar and Azhagusundarar sang Your praises in many, many ways

pañcākṣara mandirattai, neñjāra japittu vara
sañcāra manam aṭaṅkumē, aṙiyāmai maṙai
māṙumē

Heartily chanting the five syllabled mantra (na-ma-si-va-ya), calms the wavering mind and removes the veil of ignorance.

umaiyoru bākan avan
namai kākkum tandai avan
tāyin tavippai tīrttiṭavē
tāyum ānān avan... tāyum ānavan

Lord Shiva, who shares a half of Parvati (also called ardhanarishwara) is our father who protects us. He fulfills our yearning by becoming our mother (known as Tayumanavar in the town of Trichy).

nāvukkiniya mandiram – ōm namaḥ śivāya
nāḷum japippōm mandiram – ōm namaḥ śivāya
namaḥ śivāyōm namaḥ śivāyōm namaḥ śivāya

The mantra that sweetens our tongue - Om namah Sivaya. Let us always chant “Om namah Sivaya.”

iṇaiyillā īsan avan
vinai tīrkkum vimalanan avan
viṇṇum maṇṇum eṭṭā, aṇṇāmalaiyān-avan
aṇṇāmalaiyānavan

He is the Lord like no other. He removes all our sorrows. He is the Lord Annamalai (also called Arunachala in Tiruvannamalai) who pervades the entire universe.

pantaḷa rājā ayyappā (Malayalam)

pantaḷa rājā ayyappā pampāvāsā ayyappā
śabari-girīśanē ayyappā, śāntasvarūpā ayyappā

O Lord Ayyappa, king of Pandalam, Lord of Shabarimala, of serene form, you reside on the banks of the Pampa river.

pāvana pūruṣa ayyappā, pāpa vināśā ayyappā
dharmādhipanē ayyappā, pulivāhananē ayyappā

O Lord Ayyappa, pure being, destroyer of sin! You are the lord of dharma, and your vehicle is a tiger.

bhāktavatsalā ayyappā, bhūtanāyaka ayyappā
śaṅkara putrā ayyappā, mōhini putrā ayyappā

O Lord Ayyappa, you are affectionate towards your devotees, and are the leader of the bhutas. You are the son of Shankara and Parvati.

mahiṣī samhāra ayyappā, vāvaru mitrā ayyappā
śaraṇam śaraṇam ayyappā, śaraṇam śaraṇam
ayyappā

O Lord Ayyappa, you killed the demoness Mahishi, and are the friend of Vavaru. O Lord Ayyappa, we take refuge in You!

parandu virindu (Tamil)

parandu virindu niraindu viḷaṅgum
akhaṇḍa jyōtiyē
siranda marundai viraindu vazhaṅkum
ātmabōdhamē

O all-pervading and all-encompassing Divine Light! O quick! give the best medicine for Self-knowledge!

kanindu varamaruḷ malarnda mukham koṇḍa
ādinātanai
ninaindu urugiḍa toḍarndu nizhalena
varukinḍra dēvanē

Primordial Lord with a pleasing countenance, compassionate giver of boons! O Lord, You follow me like a shadow when my heart melts in thoughts of You.

kaḍaindu uḷamadai toḍuttu kavalaiyai
magizhum tūyanē
urukki akamadai jayikka tērvinai
tuṇaikku varubavanē

O Pure One, churning my heart gives You joy. You expose its anxieties and cure them permanently. O my protective companion, you make my heart one-pointed and help me pass my tests.

śiva śambhō svayambho...

O Shiva, partner of the divine Mother, the Self-emanated One!

pozhindu mazhaiyakam kuḷirndu vaḷampera
vāzhttum bhagavānē
taḍuttu āṭkoṇḍu parittu ulagiyal
sukhattai āṇḍavanē

O God, bestower of rains that cool and nourish my heart. O Ruler, You remove my tendency to hanker after lowly worldly enjoyments

jagattil jīvanai uzhattri ihalōka
sukhattai aḷippavanē
marukka ataidinam uraikkum buddhiyil
vizhippai tarubavanē

You take souls across the sufferings of this world and give true bliss. You are the One who awakens, by ever teaching us to reject worldly joys.

virittu valayinai piḍittu manadinai
vaḷaikkum īśanē
tirutti iruḷinai akattri tiraiyinai
iṇaippāy kazhalilē

O Lord, You cast the net to catch my mind. O Lord, please remove the darkness and the veil of maya. Please attach me to Your holy feet.

Pikimusta taivas (Finnish)

Pikimusta taivas, yllä öisen maan.
Kali tanssii Shivan päällä taivas verhonaan
taivas verhonaan

In pitch-black night sky above the earth. Kali dances on Shiva. The sky is her veil.

Mustat hiukset hulmuten, tumma iho loistaen
Rakkaus on aseenaan, nilkkarenkaat nilkoissaan
käy Kali tanssimaan
käy Kali tanssimaan!

Her black hair flows. Her dark skin glows. Love is her weapon. Wearing anklets on Her feet, Kali starts Her dance.

Hah hah hah hah! Hoh hoh hoh hoh!
Kali nauraa! Kali tanssii!
Hah hah hah hah! Hoh hoh hoh hoh!
Jalkojensa alla on Shivan rauha loputon
Shivan rauha loputon.

Hah hah hah hah! Hoh hoh hoh hoh! Kali is laughing, Kali is dancing! Under Her feet lies Shiva's eternal peace.

Mayan ikiyössä liekki leimahtaa.
Tiedon miekka sielun työssä, Äiti rakastaa!
Äiti rakastaa!

The sword of knowledge that uplifts my soul, flashes like lightning in the dark night of illusion. It is Mother's Love.

Kalin villi tanssi on, Shivan päällä vallaton
Asunansa aika on, Rakkaus on rajaton,
Äiti lapset pelastaa! Äiti lapset pelastaa!

Kali's dance on Shiva's chest is wild. Time is Her disguise. Her love is limitless! Mother saves Her children.

śakti bhairavi maha kāli
śakti bhairavi kāli mā
mā kāli mā kāli mā kāli mā

prabhu bin (Hindi)

prabhu bin jīvan kaisē bītā
prabhu bin jīvan kaisē bītā

How can I tell how life went on without the Lord?

prabhu kē nām ratan kō tyāgā
cōrī kar kaṅkar maiṅ bhāgā
is saude meṅ, kaun batāyē
maiṅ bāzī hārā yā jītā

Renouncing the gemstone of the Lord's name, I stole a mere pebble and ran! Can anyone tell me whether I am a loser or a winner in this deal?

jīvan bhar yahi kiyē jhamēlē
viṣayōṅ kē ras bahut uṇḍēlē
man ghaṭ phir bhī rah gayā rītā
ab jānā ik prabhu hī mītā

All my life, I messed up and poured sense pleasures into this pot called 'mind,' but it was still empty! Now I realize that the Lord is my one and only friend.

prabhu nē man mēṅ nēha jagāyā
tab hī uskī śaraṇ mēṅ āyā
prabhu kī jōt jagī jō man mēṅ
tabsē jaisē amṛt hī pītā

The Lord has awakened His love in my heart I take refuge in Him. Since the lamp of God's love is lit in my heart, I am as if drunk on nectar!

prēmadondu (Kannada)

prēmadondu hanigāgi hāttoredē
prēmagaṅgeyāde nī snēha-sindhuvādē

I yearned for a drop of love, O Mother, and You became a river, a sea of love.

iruḷallī eḍavuta nā nadedē
beḷakanu arasuta nānalede
jagavannē bēlaguva prabhēyāde nī
parama prēmada seleyādē
ammā... ammā... ammā... ammā

I was stumbling in darkness searching for light. You came as light that lit the whole world. You came as the source of pure love, O Mother.

asthiravādī lōkadalli
susthiravāda nele nīnādē
ninnaya matḍilē nannī lōkavu
vātsalya neleyū ninādе
ammā... ammā... ammā... ammā

In this ever-changing world, only you are permanent. Your lap is my world and Your motherly love my home.

nīnāru ammā? nān ariyē
nānyārammā? nīnē aritihē
nānnillavāde nīnē ellāvāde
ammā... ammā... ammā... ammā

Who are You, Mother? I don't know! Who am I? Only You know. I am no more. You are everything, Mother!

prēmattin tūlika (Malayalam)

prēmattin tūlika koṇḍu raciccu ñān
marataka maṇivarṇṇā ninde rūpam
kaṇṇunīr koṇḍu ñān neytiri katticcu
kaṇikaṇḍa nidhiyāṇen nīlavarṇṇan

O beautiful Lord, brilliant as an emerald, I painted Your portrait with the brush of my love. You are the treasure I beheld in the effulgence of the lamp lit with my tears.

hṛdayamām cippiyil karuti ñān vaccoru
jīvitamuttallo ende kaṇṇan
ghōrāndhakārattil snēhattinnoḷi tūki
vannaṇayēṇamē nandabālā – kaṇṇā
rādhāhṛdayam kavarnna cōrā

O Krishna, You are the pearl of life hidden in the treasure chest of my heart. O son of Nanda, captivator of Radha's heart, guide me through this terrible darkness with the light of Your love.

manamōhanā muraḷīdharā,
paramapuruṣā śrīkṛṣṇā

O enchanter of my heart, bearer of the flute, supreme Self, Lord Krishna!

ajñāna cōlayil nīntitaḷarumbōḷ
snēhattin kaikkumbiḷ nīṭṭumō nī?
vāṭāte tūmaṇam vīśi lasikkunna
vāṭāmalarallo ende kaṇṇan – ende
jīvande jīvanām cittacōran

I am floundering in the river of ignorance. Won't You reach out to me with Your loving hands? O Krishna, You are the evergreen blossom wafting its fragrance. O stealer of hearts, You are the soul of my life.

mīratan hṛdayatte śrīkōvilākkiya
kaṇṇā! en hṛttil viḷaṅgīṭaṇē
nīlakkaṭalin niṟamottu minnunna
nin tirumēni ñān kaṇḍiṭaṭṭe – kaṇṇā
ninnilēkk-enne nī cērttiṭaṇē

O Krishna, You made Meera's heart Your shrine. Please dwell in my heart, too. May I see Your holy form, that resembles the sparkling blue ocean. O Krishna, please draw me to You.

rāma rāma jaya (Sanskrit)

rāma rāma jaya rājārām
rāma rāma jaya sītārām

daśaratha-nandana rāma namaḥ
kausalya-tanayā rāma namaḥ
kōsala-rājā rāma namaḥ
ayōdhya-pālaka rāma namaḥ

tāṭakāntakā rāma namaḥ
munijana-sēvita rāma namaḥ
sādhu samrakṣaka rāma namaḥ
ahalyā mōcaka rāma namaḥ

trilōka-pālaka rāma namaḥ
hanumat āśrita rāma namaḥ

mahādēva priya rāma namaḥ
parama-pūruṣā rāma namaḥ

rām rām rām (Sanskrit)

rām rām rām rām rām rām, daśaratātmaja rām
rām rām
kausalya-nandana rām rām rām, dharma vigraha
rām

rājā rāmā sītā rāmā kōdaṇḍa rāmā
bhajlē rāma rāmā bhajlē rāma rāmā

raghukulōttama viśvāmitra priya tāṭaka
marddana rāmā
ahalyōdhāraka jānakījīvana lakṣmaṇa sēvita rāmā
kaikēyi priya rāmā hē dharmapālaka rām

bharata sēvita guha supūjita dānava bhañjana
rāmā
sādhu samrakṣaka jaṭāyu jīvana śabari vandita
rāmā
māruti priya hē rāmā sugriva suhṛta rām

vānara sēvita vibhīṣaṇa rakṣaka prēma sāgara
rāmā
rāvaṇa mardhaka mōkṣa dāyaka dharma
samrakṣaka rāmā
jay śrīrāmā bhajle jay śrīrāmā

śambho śaṅkara (Tamil)

śambho śaṅkara candraśēkhara namō pārvatīśā
dīna vatsala nitya sundara mahādēva dēvā

O Lord of Parvati, O Shankara, you wear a crescent moon on your forehead. You protect the downtrodden, eternally beautiful Lord of lords.

paramēśa paṇintōm nāṅkaḷ parivuṭan arulpurivāy
paśupatiyē aṭaikkalam niyē eṅkaḷai kāttiṭuvāy

We worship You, supreme Lord. Please be merciful and bless us. O Lord of cows (Pashupati), You are our sole refuge. Protect us.

ōm
hara hara harā gaṅgādhara hara
śiva śiva śivā śrī śailēśvarā

O Hara, O Shiva, O Shaileshwara, the Ganges flows from Your matted hair.

kāḷakūṭa viṣattai parukiya nīlakaṇṭanē vā – anta
viṣattin nikarām manavāsanaiyai azhittiṭuvāy
nīyē
naṭarājā patittiṭuvāy un malaraṭi en manatil
nandi pūjita niṙaittiṭuvāy maṅgaḷam ivvulakil

You swallowed the deadly 'kalakuta' poison, O blue-throated One. Please remove my vasanas which are as deadly as that poison. O Nataraja (cosmic dancer), rest Your feet in my mind. O Lord, you who are worshipped by Nandi (the bull), fill this world with auspiciousness.

ōm
hara hara harā ḍamaruka nātha
śiva śiva śivā śrī kaṇṭhēśvara

O Hara, Lord of damaru (two-sided drum), O Shiva, blue-throated Lord (who swallowed poison to save the devas and asuras).

taka taka taka taka taka taka
tāṇḍavamāṭi varuvāy naṭarājā
dhimi dhimi dhimi dhimi dhimi dhimi
tinmaikaḷai pōkkiṭuvāy śrī gaurīśā

O Nataraja, come dancing to me. Remove my negativities, O Lord of Gauri (Parvati).

tāṇḍavamāṭi varuvāy naṭarājā
tinmaikaḷai pōkkiṭuvāy śrī gaurīśā

Remove my negativities, O Lord of Gauri (Parvati).

Seigneur Krishna (French)

Seigneur krishna viens a moi
car je n'ai d'yeux que pour toi
Ote le voile qui nous sépare
depêche toi il est deja tard

Lord Krishna, come to me because I have eyes only for you. Remove the veil that separates us. Hurry, it is already late!

Tu m'as offert cette vie krishna
pour chanter ta mélodie krishna

hare rama hare rama rama rama hare hare
hare krishna hare krishna krishna krishna hare hare

O Krishna, you gave me this life that I may sing your melody. Glory to Rama, glory to Krishna!

Petit enfant malicieux
quelle joie de contempler tes jeux
Je m'oublie dans la dévotion
Quelle extase de chanter ton nom

Little mischievous child, it is such a joy to contemplate your lilas that I forget myself. It is such an ecstasy to sing your name with devotion.

Sento le onde (Italian)

Sento le onde a me sussurrare
due suoni che vibrano dentro di me

The waves whisper two sounds that vibrate inside of me.

ma om... ma om

Sillaba sacra d'Amore Divino
Ma mi pervade, a Te m'avvicino

Ma, the sacred syllable of divine love, pervades me and I come closer to You.

Ama e fà luce nell'esistenza
Diffondi la pace, tua vera essenza

Love and give light to this existence. Spread peace, your true essence.

Om è la Luce Divina che brilla
Ogni mia cellula è una scintilla

Om is shining divine light. Each of my cells is a spark.

Amma ci guida nel viaggio interiore
Canta i mantra, dimora nel cuore

Amma is guiding our inner journey. Chant Her mantras. Dwell in your heart.

Shénshèng Mŭqīn (Chinese)

Shénshèng mŭqīn zài duì wŏ shuō

The divine mother is telling me...

Wŏ de shēngmìng jiùshì qíjì
shénxìng zài wŏ de xīn
Bùyào dĕngdào yĭhòu zài yì niàn shén
Wŏ yōngyŏu de zhĭshì dāngxià
xià yī kè bùzài shŏu zhōng
shénshèng mŭqīn zài duì wŏ shuō

I'm the precious wonder of life. God is within me. Don't wait to remember God. The present moment is all I have. The next moment is not in my hands. The divine mother is telling me...

Tòngkŭ háishi kuàilè , zhè shì wŏ de xuănzé
Mò xūdùguāngyīn, zì xìng zhī guāngzhào yào wŏ
shengmu zai zhichu dadao
shengmu zai zhichu dadao

Misery or happiness, it's my choice. Don't waste your time. Let the light of the Self shine through me. Mother is showing the way, mother is showing the way...

ambe mā ambe mā
ambe mā ambe mā

Show me your real form (English)

Show me your real form.
Show me your real color.
Show me your real body.
and remove all your masks.

Some call you Allah.
You are nothing but light.
Some call you Yahveh.
You can take any form.
Some call you Buddha,
incarnate knowledge.
Some call you Jesus,
the pure compassion.

Some call you Krishna,
the king of dharma.
Some call you Guru Nanak,
the messenger of unity.
Some call you nature.
You are in the trees,
flowers, seas, clouds, and in all the animals.

Sitting in the dark (English)

Sitting in the dark, crying to the stars,
Will my mother not hear my call?
Silence all around, hiding in the clouds,
Even the moon abandons me.

Just like a child lost in a fair,
I cry for my mother to come.
I want to give up on this painful life,
but I know She won't want that.

She wants me to keep moving forward
though She knows the going is tough.
Yet I lose hope, my faith wanes.
I feel alone, angry and hurt.

Then a soft breeze caresses my face,
gently playing with my hair.
As it leaves, there lingers
the fragrance of jasmine.

Never can you leave me behind.
I have bound you to my heart.

śiva mahādēva (Sanskrit)

śiva mahādēva śiva mahādēva
śiva mahādēva śiva śambhō

nandi vāhana ḍamaruka nāthā
śūlādhārā namaḥ śivāya

namaḥ śivāya namaḥ śivāya
namaḥ śivāya namaḥ śivāya

śivāya namaḥ om harāya namaḥ om
śivāya namaḥ om mahadeva

nāgēndrahārā trinētradhārā
śiva mahādēva śiva śambhō

Somos todos um (Portuguese)

somos todos um na essencia
somos um no amor
uma luz so uma verdade so
somos um no amor
Mae oramos por um mundo melhor
somos um no amor

We are all one in essence. We are all one in love. Only one light, only one Truth. We are all one in love. Mother we pray to you, for a better world. We are all one in love.

lokah samastah sukhino bhavantu

somos todos um na essencia
somos um no amor
acorda deste sonho de ódio e do
Some um no amor

Dar uma mão para quem caiu
não há mais separação

We are all one, we are all one in love. Wake up from this dream of hate and pain. Give a hand to help the fallen one. There is no separation.

um caminho so um único destino
Somos um no amor

We are one in love -- only one path, only one destiny.

śrī rāma rāma raghurāma (Sanskrit)

śrī rāma rāma raghurāma kōdaṇḍa rāma jaya rāma
śrī rāma rāma raghurāma lōkābhirāma jaya rāma

O Lord Rama, lord of the Raghu dynasty! Victory to Lord Rama who holds the kodanda bow, and delights the whole world.

kausalya-tanaya rāma kamanīyarūpa rāma
saṅkaṭa-haraṇa rāma paṅkajalōcana rāma

He is the son of Kausalya, and his form is enchanting. He is the destroyer of sorrow. His eyes resemble lotus flowers.

daśaratha-nandana rāma daśamukha-mardana rāma
sītā-hṛdaya-nivāsa rāma pītāmbara-dhara rāma

Rama, son of Dasaratha, killed the ten-headed Ravana. He dwells in Sita's heart, and wears yellow robes.

kapikula vandita rāma sakala-kalāyuta rāma
yatijana-pūjita rāma patitōddhāraka rāma

Rama is praised by the monkey clan, and is proficient in all arts. He is worshipped by sages, and is the uplifter of the fallen.

nirupama sundara rāma niravadyāṅga rāma
kāma-nihanta rāma pāhi-dayālō rāma

Lord Rama of incomparable beauty, and handsome body! O destroyer of desire, merciful Rama, please protect us!

raghupati rāghava rāma raghukula tilaka rāma
raghupati rāghava rāma raghukula tilaka rāma

O Rama, Raghava, crest-jewel of the Raghu dynasty!

śrīśailavāsini (Sanskrit)

śrīśailavāsini śrīnāthasōdari
śrīrājarājēśvari... amba
dēvi paramēśvari

ōmkārarūpiṇi hrīmkāravāsini
śrīrājarājēśvarī... amba
ānandasandāyini

triśūladhāriṇi trilōkapālini
śrīrājarājēśvarī... amba
kāḷi kamalēśvari

parvatanandini sarvārtthakāriṇi
śrīrājarājēśvarī... amba
cinmayi brahmamayi

amba... akhilēśvari, amba... abhayaṅkari

sukhattilum (Malayalam)

sukhattilum dukhattilum
jayaparājayattilum
iḷakātta manasutān dhanyam

Blessed is the mind that is undisturbed in happiness and in sorrow, in success and failure.

svantaṅgaḷ bandhaṅgaḷ
sthānamānaṅgaḷ
veṙumoru svapnam pōle
māññupōy maṙaññiṭum
māññupōy maṙaññiṭum

One's relatives, honor and position will fade away and disappear, as if in a dream.

svayam ariyātt-avande
aṙivu-koṇḍentu phalam
avanavan anartthaṅgaḷ
varuttivekkum

Of what use is knowledge to one who doesn't know himself? He heaps sorrow and misfortune upon himself.

svayam avan vañcikkunnu
svayam avan duḥkhikkunnu
svayam avan eritīyil dahicciṭunnu

He deceives himself and brings sorrow upon himself. And finally his body is burnt to ashes in the blazing fire.

sun sun mā (Hindi)

sun sun mā sun sun mā
āj mēri bāt sun
lāgī mā lāgī mā
tērē caraṇōṅ kī dhun

O Mother, please listen to me, listen to me today. I am enraptured in songs of the glories of Your holy feet.

cānd tū cakōr mēṅ dēkh-dēkh hōuṅ dhanya
sīp huṅ tū mōtī kar dē svāti kī būnd ban
baras baras baras mujh pē svāti kī būnd ban
ban ban ban mā tū svāti kī bund ban

Though its love was never requited, the chakor bird found fullfilment in constantly gazing at the moon. May dew drops from the Swati star fall upon this mollusk that is me, and create a precious pearl [legend]. Shower such a drop of Swati on me, O Mother!

nirvāṇ cāhūṅ na mōkṣ kī rahē lagan
saṅg rahūṅ bas tērē caraṇōṅ kā dās ban
pād-paṅkajōṅ mēṅ tērē lipṭē yē bhramar man
guṇ gāyē guṇ gāyē guṇ gāyē bhramar man

I desire neither salvation nor liberation. I desire only to serve Your feet. May my fickle mind ever cling to Your lotus feet. May I ever sing the glories of Your holy feet.

samsār dēkh dēkh tapt hōyē mērā man
dēkh dēkh tērī chavi nāc uṭhē mērā man
nāc uṭhē jhūm uṭhē mērā nanhā sā man
dhin dhin dhin tak dhinādhin nācē mērā man

My mind burns in the fire of this world, but gazing upon Your form, my heart rejoices. My infant heart begins to dance, dance and rejoice!

Szukam cie w nocy (Polish)

Szukam cie w nocy szukam cie za dnia,
Szukam cie w niebie I na ziemi.
Powiedz mi Mamo czemu ja,
Nie widze ciebie w moim sercu.

I search for you night and day. I search for you in heaven and on earth. O tell me, Mother, why can't I see You in my heart?

Pokaz mi swoja twarz,
Pokaz ze ty to ja.

Show me Your face, show me that You are my Self!

Niech noc zastapi dzien,
A twoje swiatlo niech zastapi mnie.
Niech ten cichy ocean,
Wypelni twoj spiew.

May light replace darkness. May Your light replace me. May this silent ocean be filled with your sweet song.

om kali mata guru mata
ananda śiva śakti jaya mata
kali janani premamurti
kali bhavatarini dayamurti

taka dhimi taka jaṇu (Malayalam)

taka dhimi taka jaṇu taḷāṅku taka jaṇu
nṛttamāṭuk-en hṛttil nī
tām ta takajuṇu ta dhimi takajuṇu
taḷām kutaḷām-kutaḷām-kujamf
citta-sarassin saikata-bhūvil
cittacōranē vann-aṇayū

Please come and dance in the lake of my heart! O darling Krishna, stealer of my heart. Please come and dance in the lake of my heart!

attalozhiññatha mukta-śōkanāy
mugddhatanō ñān māraṭṭe
vēṇuvūti nī ende hṛttaṭam
snigdham-ākkuken śrīkṛṣṇā
kālil cilaṅkayōḍe āḍū mama hṛdi nī ānanda
naṭanam

Free me of all sorrow and let my mind be absorbed in you. Play your flute in my heart, making it shining pure, O my Krishna! Wearing your tinkling anklets, dance blissfully in my heart.

bhaktamīra-tan cittatār mudā
ninnilāyi layam ārnneṅkil
innu ñān sadā ninnil-ākuvān
nin mukhāmbujam dhyānippū
kālil cilaṅkayōḍe āḍū mama hṛdi nī ānanda
naṭanam

The heart of Meera, your great devotee, was always merged in you. And now, I constantly meditate on your lotus face to merge in you forever. Wearing your tinkling anklets, dance blissfully in my heart.

rasikarāja nin madhura vigraham
mānasāṅkaṇē vilasaṭṭe
sacala-mānasam acalamāyahō
tava padāmbujam puṇaraṭṭe
kālil cilaṅkayōḍe āḍū mama hṛdi nī ānanda
naṭanam

O Lord of bliss! May your sweet form roam in the courtyard of my radiant heart. May my restless heart be still and embrace your lotus feet. Wearing your tinkling anklets, dance blissfully in my heart.

nṛttamāḍu nī gōvinda
narttanamāḍu gōpālā

O Govinda, protector of cows, dance! O Gopala, my sweet cowherd, dance!

tām tittām tey tey (Malayalam)

tām tittām tey tey takatōm
takatittām timiti takatōm
tām tittām tey tey takatōm
takatittām timiti takatōm

itaḷ mūṭiya ceṇḍinuḷḷile
vaṇḍinum uṇḍoru katha parayān
bhōga-rasattil mayaṅgi madikkarut-
atil oru keṇiyuṇḍ-arike

A bee trapped in a flower that closed its petals has a story to tell. Do not be intoxicated in material pleasures. They are a trap.

atyantam cārattuḷḷ-oru
satyatte tēṭi-alaññu
kḷēśaṅgaḷkkaruti varuttān
śēṣiccatu svargga-kavāṭam

We wander aimlessly, searching outside for the Truth that is nearest to us. We think our burdens and sorrows will end only at the gates of heaven.

peṭṭenn-atu muṭṭi-viḷiccāl
kiṭṭum tan puṇya-phalaṅgaḷ
pēṭṭenn-atu koṭṭi aṭaccāl
kaṣṭam nūl poṭṭiya paṭṭam

However, in heaven, all we get is the results of our good actions. When these merits are exhausted, then we return to earthly existence, like a flying kite whose string has been cut.

bhōgattil pūti peruttāl
lābhakkoti pinneyum ērum
dēhattil 'ñān' ennuḷḷoru
bhāvattil bhāvi tulaykkum

When enamoured of worldly pleasures, we only desire more. Our "I" identification with the body will destroy our future (liberation).

eḷḷōḷam kaḷavuḷḷattil
uḷḷappōḷ uṇma maraykkum
uḷḷattil uḷḷoru satyam
taḷḷāt-uḷkkoḷḷaṇam ārum

The Truth remains veiled if even a tiny wickedness as small as a sesame seed remains. Do not reject the Truth within, but imbibe it and become one with it.

lōkattinu nalkān-uḷḷatu
tyāgattil neṭiya rahasyam
tyāgattāl periyoru satyam
bōdhiccāl amṛtattvam tān

We have learned the mighty secret of 'sacrifice'. When we realize our inherent Truth through sacrifice, this 'I' will become immortal!

tannana tannana (English)

tannana tannana tannanana
Kali devi, come running to me.

I pray to be a butterfly
drinking the nectar of Your heart.

Show me the flower of rainbow colors
blooming in Your heart, Kali Devi.
I never saw someone like You.
Kali Devi stay within me.

Kali devi amma kali devi kali ma
Kali devi amma kali devi kali ma

tāyē unai (Tamil)

tāyē unai ninaindu ninaindu
undan mayamāy māṙiṭa vēṇḍum

undan pādam enṭrum piṭittu
anbinil nānum uyarndiṭa vēṇḍum

Mother, I should think of You incessantly, become one with You, and see You everywhere. I should cling to your sacred feet and reach the heights in Your love.

tāyē unakku kōpamēdu
uḷḷadu anbu maṭṭumanṭrō
tāyai pōle nānum enṭrum
samanilai tannai eidiṭa vēṇḍum

Mother, You are only love. You can never be angry. O Mother, like You, let me reach a state of perfect equanimity.

sēvai enḍrum seydiṭa enakku
undan āsi kiḍaittiṭa vēṇḍum
ulagil śānti nilava vēṇḍi
enḍrum unnai vaṇaṅkiṭa vēṇḍum

Mother, bless me that I can always do seva (selfless service). May I always pray to You for the peace of the entire universe.

tellaccīra kaṭṭināvē (Telugu)

tellaccīra kaṭṭināvē kāḷī
rūpamēla mārcāvē kāḷī

O Kāḷī, you wear a white saree. Why have you changed your form?

ambā kāḷī jagadambā kāḷī

O Mother Kali, Universal Mother Kali!

pūlu cēta baṭināvē kāḷī
khaḍga mēla maricāvē kāḷī
mākai digi vaccināvē kāḷī
mammu prēmatō kaṭēvē kāḷī

O Kali, you hold flowers in your hands. Why have you forgotten your sword? O Kali You have come to earth for our sake. O Kali You have bound us with love!

kaugililō paṭināvē kāḷī
cevilōki dūrināvē kāḷī
hṛdayallō nilavavamma kāḷī
ahamu campavamma kāḷī

You hold us in your loving embrace, O Kali. You enter into us through our ears, O Kali! Please stay in our hearts, O dear Kali. Please kill our ego, O Kali!

śivaśiva aṇḍuvē kāḷī
śivuḍu ekkaḍamma kāḷī
śivunē mingitivā kāḷī
śivamē nīvukadā kāḷī

You always say, "Shiva, Shiva". O Kali, where is Shiva? Have you swallowed him up, O Kali? O Kali, You are the very embodiment of Shiva (the Absolute)!

śivāni kāḷī, bhavāni kāḷī, ambā kāḷī laḷitā kāḷī
amṛta kāḷī, ammā kāḷī ammā kāḷī ammā kāḷī
ammā kāḷī ammā kāḷī

Thank you for this life (English)

Thank you for this life,
for all that it has given.
Showing me true love,
I feel my spirits risen.

Take me home, Mother carry me
across the shore, where I am free.

Thank you for this life,
for all that it has taken.
You're standing by my side
when my world is shaken.

Thank you for this path
returning to you.
You and I are one.
Let me merge in thee.

tuḷasīmālayāy (Malayalam)

tuḷasīmālayāy kārmukil varṇṇā nin
tirumāṟilēkkenne cērttīṭumō
tuḷasīdaḷamāy ā tirupādattil
arccanāpuṣpamāy māṯṯīṭumō

O dark-hued one! Make me your *tulasi* garland, and hold me close to you. Transform me into a *tulasi* leaf that I may offer myself at your feet.

muraḷīgāyakā nin svara-mādhuriyil
oru svaramākkumō enneyum nī
allāykil nin tiru pādattil-uḷḷorā
nūpura maṇiyāy māṫṫumō nī

Dearest player of the flute, make me a melody that you play on your flute. Or make me a tinkling bell in your anklet.

tirumuṭikkeṭṭile nin mayilppīliyil
oru varṇṇamākkumō enneyum nī
alleṅkil nin tiru mēniyiluḷḷorā
cēlayil oru varṇṇamākkumō nī

Will you make me one of the colors of the peacock feather in your hair? Or will you make me one of the colors of the lovely raiment that you wear?

kaṇṇā enneyum cērkkumō nī

Will you hold me close, O Kanna?

umaye uḷḷil (Malayalam)

umaye uḷḷil ninaccirikkumbōḷ
uṣassāy-udiccu nin rūpam – eṅgum
uṇmayām śānti-svarūpē – ammē
uḷḷil niṙaykkū suśānti

As I remain absorbed in memories of Uma, Your radiant form dawns in my heart. You are the form of Truth and eternal peace, O Mother! Please fill my heart with blissful peace!

viṭarān vembunna koccarimoṭṭu-pōl
viśvam puṇarān koticcu – nitya

vimalayām prēmasvarūpē – ammē
viśvēśiyōṭ-aliyaṭṭe

Like a new bud longs to bloom, I long to embrace the universe. O Mother, eternally pure embodiment of love! Goddess of this universe, may I merge into you.

akamē tīrttoru ānanda-tantriyil
ādyamāy nādam uyartti – śuddha
ātma-bhāvattin svarūpē – ammē
āliṅganattāl aṇaykkū

You brought to life the melody of joy in the musical strings of my heart. O Mother! Hold me close. You are my pure effulgent Self.

maunamāy etti nī enne tuṇaykkumbōḷ
mānasam bhāvārdram-ākum – kālam
māykkātta satyamām sattē – ammē
mānasatāril vasikkū

You come to me as silence, and my heart grows tender. You are the unfading Truth, my essence. Please reside in my heart forever.

vāṇi sarasvati (Malayalam)

vāṇi sarasvati namōstutē
vīṇā vādini namōstutē
vidyā dāyini namōstutē

saṅgītattin dēvata nī
śāradē dēvi pālayamām

maṅgaḷa dāyini pālayamām
amṛtavarṣiṇi pālayamām

śaraṇam śaraṇam śaraṇam ammā

vēlavanē śakti (Tamil)

vēlavanē śakti vēlavanē
jñāna vēlavanē śrīmuruganē vā vā

Lord Muruga who wields a spear, come! Bestower of knowledge, come!

vēlavā vēlavā vēlavanē vā vā
vēlavā vēlavā vēlmurugā vā vā

Lord Muruga who wields a spear, come!

pārvati-nandana vēlavā vēlavā
trinētra-sutanē vēlavā vēlavā
gaṇapati-sōdara vēlavā vēlavā
śakti-svarūpananē vēlavā vēlavā

Son of Goddess Parvati, son of the three-eyed Lord Shiva, brother of Ganapati, embodiment of energy, Lord Muruga!

ṣaṇmukha dēvā vēlavā vēlavā
subrahmaṇya dēvā vēlavā vēlavā
śaravaṇa dēvā vēlavā vēlavā
śānta-svarūpananē vēlavā vēlavā

Lord Muruga, with six faces, Lord Subrahmanya, embodiment of peace, Lord Muruga!

śaktivēl murugane hara harō hara hara
jñānavēl murugane hara harō hara hara
amṛtavēl murugane hara harō hara hara

Victory to Lord Muruga who wields the spear, the Lord who grants knowledge and immortality!

veṇṇai uṇṇum (Tamil)

veṇṇai uṇṇum kaṇṇanai nān kanavil kaṇḍēnē – avan
viḷayāṭṭai kaṇḍu nānum paravasamānēn
uḷḷam paravasamānēn, uḷḷam paravasamānēn

I dreamt I saw Krishna eating butter and I was excited to see His play. My mind was elated.

māḍu mēkkyum siruvanai nān kanavil kaṇḍēnē
māya kaṇṇan endruṇarntu paravasamānēn
uḷḷam paravasamānēn, uḷḷam paravasamānēn

I saw the cowherd boy in my dream and I became excited when I realized He was Krishna. My mind was elated.

tēraiyōṭṭum kaṇṇanai nān kanavil kaṇḍēnē
avan gītai ōtum pāṅkai kaṇḍu mēysilirttēnē
uḷḷam paravasamānēn, uḷḷam paravasamānēn

I saw Krishna driving the chariot, and got chills hearing Him teach the Gita. My mind was elated.

yeṅgum kaṇṇan yetilum kaṇṇan
kaṇṇan yen vāzhvānān

inta prēmam yennuḷ malara
pittan nānānēnē
rādhē kṛṣṇa rādhē kṛṣṇa rādhē kṛṣṇa rādhē kṛṣṇā
rādhē kṛṣṇa rādhē kṛṣṇa rādhē kṛṣṇa rādhē kṛṣṇā

I see Krishna everywhere. He has become my life. I am crazy with His love blossoming inside me.

Vind de vrede (Dutch)

Vind de vrede in je hart,
Laat de zon toe in je hoofd,
Hou een glimlach op je lippen,
zelfs als je het niet gelooft

Find peace in your heart. Let light shine in your mind. Keep smiling, even when you don't feel like it.

Laat de mensen dan maar praten,
want met liefde in je hart
kun je alles overwinnen,
zelfs de allergrootste smart

Let people do their talking, with love in your heart. You can overcome even the greatest of pains.

Amma, leer ons om te lachen
met een opgeruimd gemoed.
Als je weet wie of je echt bent,
krijg je ware leeuwenmoed.

Amma, teach us to laugh, with a tidy, pure mind. If we know who we really are, we have the courage of a lion.

amma leer ons om te geven
met een liefdevol gebaar
om de wereld te genezen
kom doe mee en lach nu maar

Amma teach us to give with love, to heal the world. Let us come together and smile!

geef de ander toch jouw liefde
das het mooiste dat je kan
vraag wat 'm blij zou maken
en geef haar of hem dat dan

Give your love to others. That's your most beautiful gift. Ask what would make them happy, and give them that!

een ander blij te maken
maakt jou ook vanbinnen blij
das geen geheime kennis
is van jou en is van mij

Making someone happy makes you happy too. That is no secret knowledge. It belongs to everyone!

Vlepo thavmata (Greek)

Vlepo thavmata pantu
Sta chromata tu uranu
Sta petala tu luludiu
Na to pistepso den boro
Ke ol' afta chari sti mitera mas

I see miracles everywhere--in the colors of the sky and in the petals of a flower. I can hardly believe it. And all this, thanks to our Mother.

Elate na yiortasume
jay jay ma jay jay ma
jay jay ma jay jay ma
Elate na yiortasume
Agapi ke chara, gapi ke chara

Let's celebrate, glory to Mother! Let's celebrate, love and joy!

Vlepo thavmata mikra
Pos yelane ta pedia
Pezune anemela
Ke mirazun ti chara
Telika ine poli apla.

I see small miracles: children laughing and playing and sharing their joy. Actually life can be that simple.

Vlepo thavmata megala
Pos kratai I Amma
Olo ton kosmo stin kardia
Dini agapi ke mas traguda
Ma ti theïki I ikona afti

I see great miracles. Amma carries the whole world in her heart and gives love and sings for us. What a divine sight.

jay ma jay jay ma
Agapi ke chara

Let's celebrate, glory to Mother!

Warum suchen wir (German)

Warum suchen wir den Feind
nicht die Liebe, die uns eint?
Jenseits Glaube und Kultur
liegt uns're göttliche Natur

Why do we discriminate, choosing suffering and hate over Love? Our divine nature lies beyond caste and creed.

Shanti Salaam Pace Shalom

Peace, peace, peace, peace [in the languages of Hinduism, Buddhism, Islam, Christianity, Judaism.]

Warum seh'n wir Religion
mit Herablassung und Hohn?
welchen Namen wir auch nennen
den selben Gott wir anerkennen

Why do we view religion with condescension and scorn? We may call out any name. The God we worship is the same.

Warum seh'n wir nicht die Schönheit
in der Vielfalt dieser Welt?
Lasst uns einander lieben
in unser'n Herzen liegt der Frieden

Why can't we see beauty in the diversity in this world? Let us love each other. Peace is in our heart.

www.ingramcontent.com/pod-product-compliance
Lightning Source LLC
LaVergne TN
LVHW051730080426
835511LV00018B/2971

* 9 7 8 1 6 8 0 3 7 8 5 7 3 *